Adviser's Guide to the Tax Consequences of the Purchase and Sale of a Business

William Olson, CPA, Ph..D.

Notice to Readers

Adviser's Guide to the Tax Consequences of the Purchase and Sale of a Business does not represent an official position of the American Institute of Certified Public Accountants, and is distributed with the understanding that the author(s), editor(s), and publisher are not rendering legal, accounting, or other professional services in this publication. The views expressed are those of the author(s) and not the publisher. If legal advice or other expert assistance is required, the services of a competent professional should be sought.

Copyright © 2005 by
American Institute of Certified Public Accountants, Inc.
New York, NY 10036-8775

All rights reserved. Checklists and sample documents contained herein may be reproduced and distributed as part of professional services or within the context of professional practice, provided that reproduced materials are not in any way directly offered for sale or profit. For information about permission to copy any part of this work for redistribution or for inclusion in another document or manuscript, please call the AICPA Copyright Permissions Hotline at (201) 938-3245. A Permissions Request Form for e-mailing requests is available at www.aicpa.org by clicking on the copyright notice on any page. Otherwise, requests should be written and mailed to the Permissions Department, AICPA, Harborside Financial Center, 201 Plaza Three, Jersey City, NJ 07311-3881.

1 2 3 4 5 6 7 8 9 0 PP 0 9 8 7 6 5

ISBN 0-87051-605-1

Table of Contents

About the Author ix

Overview xi
    Introduction xi
    Organization xi

Chapter 1 Introduction to the Purchase and Sale of a Corporate Business 1-1
    Introduction 1-1

    Assets vs. Stock Purchase 1-2
        Assets Purchase 1-2
        Stock Sale 1-3
        Tax Considerations 1-3
        Non-Tax Considerations 1-4

    Taxable vs. Tax-Free 1-5
        Tax Considerations 1-6
        Non-Tax Considerations 1-6

    Summary 1-7

Chapter 2 Taxable Asset Transactions 2-1
    Objective 2-1
    Introduction 2-1

    Asset Transactions – Buyer Concerns 2-2

    Asset Transactions – Seller Concerns 2-2

    Code Sections Primarily Affecting Seller's Concerns 2-3
        Section 331 – Shareholder Tax Consequences in Corporate Liquidations 2-3
        Section 336 – Corporate Tax Consequences of Liquidation Distributions 2-8
        Section 1245 – Character of Gain 2-8
        Section 1250 – Recapture of Excess Depreciation on Real Property 2-9

Section 453 – Installment Sales 2-9

Section 1060 – Allocation of Purchase Price 2-11
    Allocation of Purchase Price to Individual Assets Prior to Tax Reform Act (TRA) of 1986 2-11
    Section 1060's Rules 2-12
    Allocation of Sales/Purchase Price 2-14
    Effect of a Written Agreement Between the Parties 2-17
    Subsequent Adjustment 2-17
    Reporting Requirements 2-17
    Acquisition Related Costs 2-17

Summary 2-18

Case Study 2-1 2-18

    Case Study 2-1 – Dodger Manufacturing Corporation 2-18
    Case Study 2-1 – Questions & Answers 2-20

IRS Form 8594 2-25

Chapter 3 Purchases Involving Intangible Assets 3-1

    Objective 3-1
    Introduction 3-1

Background 3-1

Separable and Valuable Intangibles – Pre-Revenue Reconciliation Act (RRA) of 1993 3-2

Revenue Reconciliation Act of 1993 – Amortization of Intangible Assets 3-3
    Workforce 3-4
    Information Base 3-5
    Customer-Based Intangible 3-5
    Supplier-Based Intangible 3-6
    Know-How 3-6
    Government License 3-7
    Franchise, Trademark or Trade Name 3-7
    Excluded Assets 3-7
    Special Rules Concerning Section 197 Intangibles 3-8
    Tax Planning 3-9

Summary 3-10

Case Study 3-1 3-10
    Case Study 3-1 – Dodger Manufacturing (cont.) – Intangible Assets 3-10
    Case Study 3-1 – Dodger Manufacturing (cont.) – Questions & Answers 3-10

Chapter 4 Taxable Stock Transactions 4-1

Objective 4-1
Introduction 4-1

Taxable Stock Sale vs. Taxable Asset Sale 4-2

Section 338 – Treating Stock Purchases as Asset Purchases 4-2
Requirements for Section 338 Treatment 4-3
Old Target's Assets Sale to New Target 4-3
Primary Drawbacks of the Section 338 Election 4-3

The Section 338(h)(10) Alternative 4-4
New Selling Corporation's Responsibilities on a Target's Stock Sale 4-4
Tax Consequences to Acquirer and Seller 4-5
When to Use the Election 4-6
Allocation and Reporting Requirements 4-6

Section 338 Regulations 4-7

Summary 4-7

Case Study 4-1 4-8
Case Study 4-1 – Dodger Manufacturing (cont.) 4-8
Case Study 4-1 – Dodger Manufacturing (cont.) Questions & Answers 4-8

Chapter 5 Carryover of Tax Attributes 5-1

Introduction 5-1

Section 382 5-1
Owner Shifts 5-2
Equity Structure Shifts 5-2
Testing Periods 5-2
Losses Limited by Section 382 5-3
Five-Percent Shareholders 5-5
Impact If Section 382 Applies 5-7
Other Rules 5-8
Recognition of Built-in Gains and Losses 5-8
Section 383 5-9
Separate Return Limitation Years ("SRLYs") 5-9

Section 269 5-10
Determining Whether Section 269 Applies 5-10
Section 269(b) 5-11

Section 384 5-11

Stock Acquisitions 5-12
Asset Acquisitions 5-12
Other Considerations 5-12

Summary 5-13

Case Study 5-1 5-14
Case Study 5-1 – Mad Max Electronics Co. 5-14
Case Study 5-1 – Mad Max Electronics Co—Questions & Answers. 5-14

Chapter 6 Taxable Acquisitions Involving Sole Proprietorships, S Corporations, Partnerships, and LLCs 6-1

Objectives 6-1
Introduction 6-1

Acquisitions from a Sole Proprietorship 6-1

Acquisition of a Business from an S Corporation 6-2

Purchase of S Corporation's Assets 6-3
Passive Income Limitation 6-3
Gain on Asset Sale 6-3

A Purchaser Acquires the S Corporation's Stock 6-4
Potential Termination of the S Election 6-4
Tax Impact 6-4
Asset Versus Stock Sale 6-5

Acquisitions Involving Partnerships 6-6

Purchase of Assets from a Partnership 6-6
Consequences to the Selling Partnership 6-6
Consequences to the Purchaser 6-7

Purchase of a Partnership Interest 6-7
Consequences to the Seller of a Partnership Interest 6-7
Consequences to the Purchaser of a Partnership Interest 6-10
Consequences to the Continuing Partners and the Partnership 6-12
Principal Consequences 6-12

Limited Liability Companies 6-14
Background 6-14
Acquisition of a Business from a LLC 6-15

Summary 6-15

Chapter 7 Federal Income Tax Reporting Requirements 7-1

    Objective 7-1

  Asset Purchases 7-1

  Stock Purchases 7-2
    Form 8023 7-2
    Form 8883 7-3

  Sale or Exchange of Certain Partnership Interests 7-3

  Section 382 and Loss Corporation Information Disclosure 7-4

  Forms 8308, 8023, and 8883 7-7

Chapter 8 Other Acquisition-Related Issues 8-1

  Objectives 8-1
  Introduction 8-1

  Treatment of Expenses Incurred in an Acquisition 8-1
    Expensing vs. Capitalizing 8-2
    Takeovers: The Target's Tax Treatment 8-2
    Position of the Courts 8-3
    Position of the IRS 8-4
    Tax Planning Comment 8-5

  Compensation Issues 8-5
    Golden Parachute Payments 8-6
    Greenmail Payments 8-10

  Summary 8-12

Chapter 9 Ethics Focus: Taxation 9-1

  Ethics Overview 9-1
  Key Ethical Dilemmas and Judgment Calls 9-1
  Addressing Ethical Dilemmas 9-2
  Available Resources 9-3
  Legislative Developments 9-4

Appendix A: Due Diligence Checklist.. **A-1**

**Appendix B : Summary of Provisions of the Working Families Tax Relief Act of 2004
and the American Jobs Creation Act of 2004**...................................... **B-1**

Glossary of Terms.. **G-1**

Index.. **I-1**

About the Author

William H. Olson, Ph.D., CPA, received his Ph.D. in Accounting, with a specialization in Taxation, from the University of North Texas. He is the author of numerous publications on tax, accounting and financial matters, and has taught as an Adjunct Professor at several universities. Dr. Olson's professional experience includes senior positions in both public accounting and industry. He is currently a Principal with UHY Mann Frankfort Stein and Lipp Advisors, Inc., in Houston, Texas.

UHY Advisors, Inc., (www.uhy-us.com) formerly Centerprise Advisors, Inc., is the nation's 15th largest accounting, tax and consulting firm with over 20 offices in the United States and 148 affiliate offices worldwide.

UHY Advisors, Inc. provides a wide range of professional and business services, including accounting, tax and business advisory services, in addition to group health and life insurance services.

UHY Advisors, Inc. and its professional services subsidiaries are independent members of Urbach Hacker Young International Limited, a UK-based organization of independent and separate firms that has more than 4,000 professionals operating in 148 offices in 50 countries. Urbach Hacker Young International Limited is the result of the 1987 combination of Urbach Kahn & Werlin of New York and Hacker Young of London.

Overview

Introduction

This book is designed to introduce participants to the federal income tax considerations relevant to the *taxable* purchase and sale of a business. This includes the special rules that apply to acquisitions involving S corporations, limited liability companies (LLCs), and partnerships. It also addresses the reporting of these transactions and the tax treatment of acquisition expenses. The focus is on taxable transactions. Acquisitions accomplished through tax-free reorganizations are not discussed in this book.

Organization

Chapter 1—In initially analyzing the sale or purchase of a business, many tax and non-tax issues must be considered. This chapter reviews these items, which are important in determining whether a transfer of assets or stock is preferable.

Chapter 2—This chapter analyzes various tax considerations in a taxable asset acquisition from a "C" or regular corporation. Some of the concepts discussed include the following: benefits of an installment sale; allocation of lump asset sales price; and liquidating the corporate business as part of the sale.

Chapter 3—This chapter specifically discusses the types of *intangible* assets that might be acquired in a business acquisition and the tax treatment and basis determination of these intangibles. The rules under Internal Revenue Code (IRC) Section 197, which permit amortization of certain intangibles (including goodwill) over 15 years are discussed.

Chapter 4—This chapter analyzes taxable stock transactions. Some topics discussed include §338 and §338(h)(10) elections.

Chapter 5—This chapter discusses the carryover of tax attributes [e.g., net operating losses (NOLs) and tax credits, etc.] in a stock acquisition.

Chapter 6—This chapter discusses the tax consequences when an S corporation, partnership, sole proprietorship, or LLC is involved in an acquisition transaction.

Adviser's Guide to Tax Consequences of the Purchase and Sale of a Business

Chapter 7—This chapter summarizes the reporting requirements for the various types of acquisitions discussed in this book.

Chapter 8—This chapter discusses the treatment of acquisition-related expenses, such as investment banking fees, attorneys' fees, accountants' fees, and commitment fees. In addition, it discusses certain types of compensation payments, such as golden parachute payments and greenmail payments, and the imposition by Congress of excise taxes in order to discourage them.

Chapter 9—This chapter highlights some of the more common ethical dilemmas that practitioners might encounter in the course of their tax practice.

In addition, the book provides a sample due diligence checklist in Appendix A, "Due Diligence Checklist," and highlights current legislative developments in Appendix B, "Summary of Provisions of the Working Families Tax Relief Act of 2004 and the American Jobs Creation Act of 2004."

Chapter 1

Introduction to the Purchase and Sale of a Corporate Business

Introduction

In making an acquisition or disposition of a corporate business, a thorough analysis is necessary to adequately advise clients and senior company management. Taxpayers selling a business must ensure that all tax, accounting, and operational considerations have been addressed.

In this chapter, we will mention a number of potential considerations in the purchase of a business operated in corporate form and then discuss these issues in greater detail in the remainder of the book. We will also discuss acquisitions of businesses operated in other forms, to include S corporations, partnerships, sole proprietorships, and LLCs (limited liability companies).

The seller should attempt to foresee what items and business areas will be important to a potential buyer. For example, the buyer of a corporate business relies greatly on the seller's financial statements. To a large extent the sales price is determined on the historical information found in these financial statements. If the seller's financial statements have never been audited, or have not been audited within the past six months, an audit should be considered to allow for an accurate presentation of current financial information.

Some other items that may be important in the sale of a corporate business include the following:

- The payment record of federal taxes;
- State income tax;
- Sales tax;
- Franchise tax;
- Stamp and transfer taxes;
- Contractual obligations;

- Title restrictions on property;

- Registration of patents; trademarks; trade names and copyrights;

From the buyer's standpoint, appropriate "due diligence" procedures must be performed to ensure the transaction is structured properly, the purchase price is not overstated, and that all potential liabilities have been identified. Appendix A, "Due Diligence Checklist" highlights areas of concern that practitioners should be familiar with before finalizing any agreement.

Tax Structuring Decisions

From a tax perspective two considerations are of paramount importance:

- Should the transaction be structured as a sale of *stock* or *assets*?

- Should the transaction be structured as a *taxable* or *tax-free* acquisition?

Categories of Acquisitions

Acquisitions will therefore fall into one of the following categories:

- Taxable – Asset (discussed later in the book).

- Taxable – Stock (discussed later in the book).

- Tax-Free – Asset (this involves reorganization tax rules, which are not covered in this book).

- Tax-Free – Stock (this involves reorganization tax rules, which are not covered in this book).

Assets vs. Stock Purchase

Assets Purchase

For the *buyer* of a business an acquisition of assets is generally preferable to the acquisition of stock. For example, an asset acquisition allows the buyer to purchase specific assets of the corporation. The segregation of specific assets with a stock sale is difficult.

The buyer can also "step-up" the tax basis of the assets in an asset purchase to increase depreciation deductions. Furthermore, an asset acquisition allows the buyer to purchase the assets without regard to contingent or unknown liabilities. However, certain tax detriments are associated with an asset purchase. Asset purchases are discussed in Chapter 2, "Taxable Asset Transactions."

Stock Sale

For the *seller* of a business a *stock* sale is generally preferable to an asset sale. A stock sale is generally a simpler transaction to consummate. The sale of stock by the shareholders generally results in a capital gain, while the sale of assets by the corporation can result in significant ordinary income. Furthermore, unlike a stock sale, an asset sale triggers both a corporate level tax and a shareholder level tax. Stock purchases are discussed later in this book.

The above comments are generalizations. There may be valid business reasons why, for example, a buyer might desire a stock purchase. The tax consequences of the different modes of acquisitions are discussed more fully in the following chapters. A brief summary of various tax considerations follows. These considerations should be considered collectively in deciding the best way to structure a transaction.

Tax Considerations

Basis of Assets

In an asset purchase the buyer receives a tax basis equal to the purchase price. In a stock purchase the buyer receives a tax basis in the stock acquired. Without a §338 election (discussed in Chapter 5, "Carryover of Tax Attributes"), a stock purchaser assumes a "carryover" of basis in the assets acquired. When the buyer acquires assets with value in excess of their historical tax basis, an asset acquisition is generally more favorable, because it allows the new tax basis to be "stepped up" to the current fair market value. When the buyer acquires assets with a tax basis greater than their value, a stock acquisition may be more favorable (to avoid a basis "stepdown").

Tax Attributes

A careful analysis of the selling company's tax attributes must be made by the buyer to determine if they would be favorable or unfavorable to the purchaser. In an *asset* purchase the tax attributes do *not* carry over to the purchaser. Therefore, the seller's tax attributes (such as loss and credit carryovers, tax basis of assets, earnings and profits, recapture liabilities, etc.) should be considered. In a *stock* purchase the tax attributes of the acquired (target) corporation generally remain with the company when ownership is transferred to the acquirer.

However, as discussed in Chapter 6, "Taxable Acquisitions Involving Sole Proprietorships, S Corporations, Partnerships, and LLCs," there are restrictions on the carryover of certain attributes even in a stock acquisition.

For example: In an asset purchase the corporation's earnings and profits do not carry over to the buyer. This may be advantageous to the buyer, since the buyer can incorporate the acquired assets and make distributions that may not be characterized as dividends from preacquisition earnings and profits.

Outstanding Installment Receivables

Uncollected receivables that were reported on the installment method at the time of origination are triggered into the seller's income on an asset sale. In a stock sale the installment obligations are not accelerated and the buyer reports the income and pays taxes as the collections are made.

Double Tax

A corporation's sale of assets and subsequent distribution of cash of the net proceeds to the shareholders results in a tax at both the corporate and shareholders' level. A sale of stock only triggers a single level of tax (to the shareholders). This concept is discussed more fully later in the book.

Personal Holding Company

If a company sells substantially all of its assets, retains the proceeds and does not liquidate, the corporation *could* be classified as a personal holding company with the negative tax consequences associated with the classification. The sale of stock by the shareholders will not have this result.

S Corporation Status

The involvement of an S Corporation in an acquisition can involve specific rules applicable to S Corporations. These are discussed later in the book.

Partnerships and LLCs

The acquisition of businesses operated in partnership or LLC form can involve special rules. These are also discussed later in the book.

Non-Tax Considerations

In addition to complex federal income tax considerations, the purchase or sale of a corporate business involves many legal and financial considerations.

Some of the *nontax* considerations involved in determining whether to sell assets or stock include the following:

- An asset purchase allows the buyer to choose which assets are to be acquired.

- A stock purchase is generally easier to consummate.

- A stock purchaser assumes all unknown and contingent liabilities of the acquired corporation.

Introduction

- Loan covenants may restrict a company's ability to dispose of assets.

- An asset sale can involve the assignment of contractual rights (lease, franchise, etc.) that may require the consent of the contracting party. This is usually not the case with a stock purchase.

- An asset sale may terminate negotiated collective bargaining agreements between a union and the company.

- A stock purchase should not affect any favorable unemployment or worker's compensation insurance ratings.

- An asset purchaser may not receive the right to use the corporate name of the seller.

- An asset purchaser has the ability to place the assets in another company that is in a different state of incorporation, thereby changing the state of incorporation for the assets. A stock purchaser must go through another transaction (i.e., liquidation or reorganization) to accomplish this.

- The purchase of stock may require additional filings with the Securities and Exchange Commission (SEC).

- The sale of substantial assets by a corporation generally requires shareholder approval and may, for dissenting shareholders, require appraisal rights.

- A sale of stock terminates the shareholders' interest in the company.

- The purchase of stock may require the purchaser to assume the liability for an underfunded employee benefit plan.

Taxable vs. Tax-Free

In addition to deciding whether the transaction should be a stock or an asset acquisition, a decision must be made to determine whether the transaction can be (should be) structured as tax-free or taxable.

- *In a taxable acquisition*:

    The sale of the stock (or assets) of a company can generate an immediate tax to the shareholders (and in the case of an asset sale, to the corporation itself). A taxable acquisition generally involves cash or notes as consideration.

- *In a tax-free acquisition*:

    The assets or stock of a company will generally be acquired as a §368 tax-free reorganization. The purchaser will generally receive a carryover basis in the assets acquired, and generally neither the shareholders nor the company will recognize an immediate gain or loss on the disposition. The consideration given to the sellers will include (or be limited to) the stock/securities of the purchaser (or an affiliate). Reorganizations are not discussed in detail in this book.

Tax Considerations

Seller's Tax Basis in Assets

The choice between a taxable and tax-free transaction will be influenced by the cost recovery deductions available to the buyer. If the current tax basis of the assets is higher than the purchase price, a *tax-free* transaction that preserves this higher tax basis would generally be preferred by the buyer.

To the contrary, a high tax basis in the assets will make the seller more inclined to sell assets in a taxable transaction, since his potential gain is minimized.

Seller's Tax Attributes

One motive in making a tax-free asset or stock acquisition is the potential acquisition of a company's net operating losses (NOLs), capital loss carryovers, etc. While such attributes are available (subject to certain limitations) following a stock sale or tax-free reorganization, they will *not* be available to the buyer in a taxable asset sale.

Installment Reporting/Deferral

A taxable sale of stock or assets can sometimes allow the seller to report the sale on the installment method, thus reducing the seller's immediate tax liability. This can allow *some amount* of tax deferral in a taxable transaction.

A tax-free transaction can *indefinitely* defer gain recognition on the part of the target's shareholders. Specifically, a tax-free reorganization defers the recognition of income for shareholders, since they generally take a basis in the stock received equal to the basis in the stock they surrender. Any gain inherent in the stock received is deferred until it is sold.

Non-Tax Considerations

Some of the non-tax considerations in choosing between a taxable and tax-free transaction include the following:

Introduction

- A tax-free transaction may not allow the seller to convert his/her realized gain to cash immediately, because of potential tax (continuity of interest) or SEC [§16(b)] complications, requiring some period of post-disposition ownership.

- A taxable asset purchase may require large amounts of selling expenses and time to transfer assets. A statutory tax-free transaction may substantially reduce the necessary time and costs.

- State merger or reorganization laws may impose restrictions on some types of tax-free acquisitions.

The emphasis in this book is on *taxable* stock and asset transactions ("purchase" transactions). Tax-free acquisitions and dispositions (reorganizations) are not covered in this book.

Summary

There are numerous tax considerations in a corporate acquisition or disposition that will vary with the form of the transaction (asset vs. stock, and taxable vs. tax-free). Well advised buyers and sellers should seek to structure the transaction in the most advantageous manner.

There are also numerous non-tax considerations to be evaluated in structuring a transaction. Since these non-tax considerations may overshadow the tax consequences, a tax adviser should be familiar with their ramifications.

The following chapters explore in greater detail the concepts introduced in this chapter.

Chapter 2

Taxable Asset Transactions

Objective

This chapter will explain the tax consequences that buyers and sellers must consider when evaluating a corporate asset transaction.

Introduction

This chapter discusses the tax consequences that sellers and buyers of a corporate business must consider when evaluating a corporate *asset* transaction. The discussion focuses on a business owned by a "C" or regular corporation. It will include general tax consequences of acquisitions and special considerations when a business is acquired from such a corporation. Later in this book, we will address somewhat different consequences when assets are acquired from other owners, such as an S corporation, sole proprietor, partnership, or limited liability company (LLC).

If the sale of a business enterprise is structured as an asset disposition, there are two possible methods to consummate the transaction:

- The corporation can distribute all of its *assets* to its shareholders in a liquidating distribution. Following the distribution, the shareholders can sell the assets to the acquiring party; or

- The corporation can sell the assets to the acquiring party and distribute the proceeds to its shareholders in a liquidating distribution.

The economics of the above situations are similar, and the tax consequences are also similar. Either of the above alternatives involves tax consequences at both the corporate and shareholder levels. Either structure will also usually involve the complete liquidation of the corporation.

Note. It is possible that the corporation could sell *most* of its assets, distribute the proceeds to its shareholders, but not liquidate. In this scenario the corporation would be kept "alive" as a "shell" corporation (assuming it did not have another business to operate). However, this can expose the corporation to various problems, including the onerous personal holding company tax. For this and other reasons, selling shareholders usually structure an asset sale to include the complete liquidation of their corporation, and the following discussion assumes a corporate liquidation.

Asset Transactions — Buyer Concerns

There are several reasons why the buyer may prefer to directly acquire the target corporation's *assets*.

- An outright asset purchase allows the buyer to allocate the purchase price to the target's underlying assets. This provides additional tax deductions (e.g., through depreciation and amortization) if the fair market value of the assets is higher than the seller's historic tax basis.

- A stock purchase will not allow the stock's purchase price to be reflected in a stepped-up asset basis, unless a §338 election is made. However, as discussed later in the book, §338 elections are generally no longer viable.

- Asset acquisitions prevent the buyer from acquiring unknown or contingent target liabilities. Only liabilities specifically assumed by the buyer (or to which the assets transferred are encumbered) are of specific concern. This is not true of stock acquisitions.

However, an asset purchase also has potential drawbacks for the buyer. For example, the target's desirable tax attributes [e.g., net operating loss (NOL) carryforwards and credits] do not follow the assets. In a stock acquisition, subject to certain limitations, the buyer gains access to these desirable tax attributes.

Asset Transactions – Seller Concerns

Generally, regardless of whether the corporation distributes its assets or sells its assets and distributes the net proceeds to its shareholders in complete liquidation, the *shareholders* recognize gain or loss for the excess of the fair market value of the distributed assets over their stock basis [§331].

At the *corporate* level the corporation pays tax on any gain realized on the assets sold. Also, if the assets are distributed directly to the shareholders in complete liquidation, the assets are *deemed sold* [§336], and a corporate tax is triggered.

Regardless of whether corporate assets are sold by the shareholders (after distribution) or directly by the corporation, §1060 must be considered. Section 1060 imposes restrictions on how to allocate the sales proceeds, which will impact the amount and nature of the gain or loss recognized. These allocation rules also dictate how the buyer must allocate the purchase price, which will impact the buyer's after-tax returns from the acquisition.

The following is a discussion of Internal Revenue Code Sections (§) that impact the seller's tax consequences in an asset sale.

These include the following:

- §331;
- §336;
- §1245;
- §1250; and
- §453.

Although these provisions are of primary importance to the seller, buyers should also be aware of them to assess the seller's tax consequences.

The chapter concludes with a discussion of §1060. This section impacts the *seller's gain or loss* recognition and the *buyer's tax basis* in the assets.

Code Sections Primarily Affecting Seller's Concerns

Section 331 – Shareholder Tax Consequences in Corporate Liquidations

Section 331 provides that amounts distributed to shareholders in corporate liquidations are generally treated by the recipients as receipts from the sale of the stock. All realized gain or loss (the difference between fair market value and tax basis) is recognized.

Section 331 is relevant whether the assets are distributed by the corporation to the shareholders in liquidation (who sell them) *or* if the corporation sells the assets and distributes the cash proceeds in liquidation to the shareholders.

The following is an outline of the more important §331 provisions:

Character of Gain or Loss to a Shareholder

Amounts received by a shareholder in a corporate liquidation distribution are treated as in exchange for the stock [§331(a)]. If the stock is a capital asset (which it usually is), long-term or short-term capital gain or loss results.

Amount of Gain or Loss to a Shareholder

All *realized gain or loss* is recognized [§1001(c)]. *Realized gain or loss* equals the amount received, minus the adjusted stock basis [§1001(a)]. The "amount realized" equals the money received, plus the fair market value of the other property received, minus the liabilities assumed or taken subject to [§1001(b)].

Receipt of Property Other Than Money

Subject to the comments below regarding "open" transactions, all property received is included in the amount realized at its fair market value. Therefore, a shareholder may be cash out-of-pocket after taxes are paid (i.e., shareholders may have to sell the distributed noncash assets to pay the tax on the distribution).

- *Distributed Property that Is Difficult to Value — The "Open Transaction"* — A potential problem concerns the valuation of contract rights to receive indefinite amounts that are based on contingencies, claims in dispute, etc., or distributed properties without a market (i.e., assets with speculative value).

   The "open transaction" doctrine states that where an asset does not have an ascertainable value, there is no fair market value placed on it. Instead, the transaction is treated as "open," future proceeds are applied first against the basis of the stock, and any excess is treated as a capital gain from the sale of stock (*Burnet v. Logan*, 283 U.S. 404, 1931).

   Except in "rare and extraordinary" cases, the IRS requires the valuation of contracts and claims, which are to receive indefinite amounts of income (*Rev. Rul. 58402*, 19582 CB 15). The IRS argues that all property has an ascertainable value, except in rare circumstances.

- *Results If Distributed Claim Is Fixed* — In this case the claim or contract is included at the fair market value in determining the amount realized on liquidation. The basis of the contract or claim becomes fair market value [§334(a)].

   If collections are in excess of the basis of the claim or the contract, ordinary income is realized since there is no sale or exchange. Similarly, if collections are *less* than the basis of the claim or contract, an ordinary loss is realized since there is no sale or exchange. (The IRS has argued in some cases for capital loss treatment.)

Treatment of Contingent Corporate Liabilities Distributed in Liquidation

The amount realized on liquidation is reduced by the definite known liabilities assumed (or taken subject to) by a shareholder.

The legal doctrine of "transferee liability" indicates that the shareholder of a liquidated corporation is obligated to its creditors for an amount equal to the net value of the assets he receives in liquidation.

Contingent or unknown corporate liabilities paid by a shareholder in a year *following* the liquidation are generally deductible as a *capital loss* in the year of payment. The rationale is that the payment relates to the liquidation, i.e., reduces the capital gain or increases the capital loss (*Arrowsmith v. Comm.*, 344 U.S. 6, 1952).

Tax Basis of Property Received in a §331 Liquidation

The shareholder's basis of property received in liquidation is the fair market value on the distribution date [§334(a)]. The basis is the same even if the property is encumbered by a liability.

Example 2-1

A building received in liquidation has a fair market value of $100,000 and is encumbered by a mortgage of $20,000.

The building's basis to the shareholder is $100,000.

Note: Special rules apply if the liability is in excess of the property's fair market value.

The property's *holding period* commences on the date the property is received (since the distribution is a taxable transaction).

The tax character of the asset to the recipient shareholder (e.g., capital asset, §1231 asset, or inventory) depends on the shareholder's relationship to the property and his intent in holding the asset (*ACRO Mfg.*, 334 F2d 40 964 CA6).

Corporate and Shareholder Liquidation Expenses

Expenses paid by the corporation prior to the filing of its final tax return are generally deductible if associated with the liquidation (attorney's fees, filing fees, etc.) (*Rev. Rul.* 77204, 19771 CB 40).

As mentioned previously, liabilities paid by former shareholders relating to property received in the liquidation generally result in a capital loss to the shareholder [*Arrowsmith*, 344 US 1 (1952)].

Expenses incurred by a liquidating corporation, which will benefit a shareholder subsequent to the liquidation, should not be deducted by the corporation on its final return. Expenses incurred by a liquidating corporation that benefit both the company and the shareholders, post-liquidation, may be prorated between the corporation and the shareholders [§164(d)].

Illustration: Section 331 in a Taxable Liquidation

Example 2-2

Consider the complete liquidation of SEMI CORP, which has the following balance sheet:

<u>Assets</u>

Cash	$ 35,000
Land and Building (net of Straight-line Depreciation)	200,000
Total Assets	**$235,000**

<u>Liabilities and Capital</u>

Mortgage	$ 10,000
Capital Stock	200,000
Retained Earnings	25,000
Total Liabilities and Capital	**$235,000**

The fair market value of the land and building is $2 million.

Mack's Basis in Stock and Gain before Taxes

Mack, a 60% shareholder, has a basis in his stock (which he has held for 2 years) of $120,000.

For simplicity of calculation, assume a 20% capital gain tax rate.

On the complete liquidation of SEMI, Mack has a gain before taxes of $1,095,000, computed as follows (assuming Mack and the other shareholders will hold a joint interest in the land and building)

Amount realized

Cash	$ 21,000
Land and Building (60%)	1,200,000
Mortgage	(6,000)
Amount realized	1,215,000
Less: Basis of stock	(120,000)
Gain before taxes	$1,095,000

Tax Consequences

There will be two separate taxes to be paid.

- The corporation will have to pay a tax of 34% on the appreciation of assets distributed as a result of the repeal of the General Utilities doctrine (see discussion below). Mack will have to pay his proportionate share of this tax.

- Mack will have to pay a tax at a rate of 20% on his gain from the distribution, which will take into account the corporate tax.

Thus, a tax of 47.2% in effect must be paid on the appreciated property. This is 34% + 13.2% (balance of 66% x 20%).

This would produce the following taxes:

Property distributed:
Cash (less mortgage satisfied)	$ 5,000 @ 20.00%	$ 3,000
Land and building	1,080,000 @ 47.2%	509,760
	$1,095,000	$512,760

Tax consists of the following:
Corporate tax (1,080,000 @ 34%)	$367,200
Individual tax [(1,095,000 minus 367,200) x 20%]	145,560
	$512,760

Mack is net cash out-of-pocket after paying the tax (since he only receives $21,000 in cash, which is much less than the tax due).

Mack's basis for his interest in the land and building is $1,200,000 (fair market value at the date of distribution).

Adviser's Guide to Tax Consequences of the Purchase and Sale of a Business

Tax Planning: Multiple Distributions

Corporations can spread the shareholders' gain on a §331 liquidation over more than one year by making several distributions. Cost can be recovered before any gain is recognized (*Rev. Rul. 68348*, 19682 CB 141). However, a constructive receipt of assets may occur when the plan of liquidation calls for a distribution on a certain date (*Rev. Rul. 80177*, 19802 CB 236). Also, the corporation may be a personal holding company (with disadvantageous tax consequences) during the liquidation period.

Section 336 — Corporate Tax Consequences of Liquidation Distributions

Section 336 generally provides that gain or loss is recognized by a liquidating corporation on the distribution of its property in complete liquidation. Certain special rules and exceptions are provided (e.g., §332 liquidations of a subsidiary into its parent). This generally insures a "double" level of taxation on distributions to shareholders [once at the corporate (distributor) level and again at the shareholder (distributee) level].

Section 336(d) provides special rules that can limit loss recognition in certain cases. This section provides that a loss will not be recognized in certain liquidating distributions of property to a "related person" (within the meaning of §267) and in certain liquidating distributions of property acquired in carryover basis transactions.

Section 1245 – Character of Gain

This section provides that gain on the sale or other disposition of depreciable business personal property is treated as ordinary income to the extent of depreciation allowed or allowable. The remainder of any gain is taxed as long-term gain under §1231 (providing that there are no offsetting §1231 losses). Section 1231(c) provides that any net §1231 gain will be treated as ordinary income to the extent of the taxpayer's (or predecessor taxpayer) un-recaptured net §1231 losses for the five most recent prior years beginning after December 31, 1981.

Under §1245 ordinary income may result from the recapture of depreciation on property placed in service prior to 1981. For property placed in service after 1980 and subject to accelerated cost recovery system (ACRS) or modified accelerated cost recovery system (MACRS) methods, the amount recaptured is the claimed recovery allowances, plus any amounts expensed in lieu of ACRS (MACRS) allowances under §179 ($18,500 maximum for years beginning in 1998).

The amount treated as ordinary income under §1245 is the lesser of:

- The excess of the fair market value of the property over its adjusted basis, or

- The depreciation taken (for pre1981 property), or the recovery allowances and §179 expensed portion (for post1981 property).

Taxable Asset Transactions

Section 1250 – Recapture of Excess Depreciation on Real Property

Under §1250, for property acquired before 1981, ordinary income may result from the recapture of excess depreciation taken on depreciable real property. The amount of ordinary income, similar to §1245 recapture, is the lesser of the gain or excess depreciation allowed or allowable.

For ACRS real property acquired after 1980, the recapture rules apply differently for commercial real property and for residential real property:

- *For commercial property*, where the 15-, 18-, or 19-year accelerated recovery method is used, the gain constitutes ordinary income to the extent of all previously claimed recovery allowances. This is similar to the §1245 recapture rules. If the straight-line ACRS method was elected, there was no recapture prior to the Tax Equity and Fiscal Responsibility Act of 1982 (TEFRA), regardless of whether the recovery period selected was 15, 18 or 19, 35, or 45 years.

- *For residential real estate*, if the 15-, 18-, or 19-year accelerated recovery period was used, only the excess of the amount available under the straight-line method using a 15-, 18-, or 19-year recovery period was recaptured and taxed as ordinary income to the extent of gain. If the straight-line ACRS method was selected for residential real property, no recapture resulted.

    For dispositions of §1250 property after 1982, 15% of the amount by which the gain recapturable, if §1245 applied, exceeds the gain recaptured under §1250 will be "recaptured" under §1250 and treated as ordinary income. For dispositions after 1984 the recapture percentage is 20% [§291(a)(1)].

    For installment sales of property §1245 and 1250 depreciation recapture amounts must be included in income in the year of the installment sale, irrespective of any collections in that year.

    For MACRS real property all depreciation is computed on the straight-line method and consequently, there is no depreciation recapture except to the extent that §291 applies. In addition, because of the longer life of the property for the alternative minimum tax, there may be additional tax for alternative minimum tax (AMT) purposes.

Section 453 – Installment Sales

This section provides that by using an installment sale, the sellers may pay tax on the gain when and as they receive payments.

An installment sale is defined as

> A disposition of property where at least one payment is to be received after the close of the taxable year in which the disposition occurs.

The installment method automatically applies to certain prescribed transactions (e.g., sales other than those of publicly traded stock), unless the seller elects out of the method. When the installment method is applicable, tax is paid only on the ratable profit percentage applied to each year's payment.

- All depreciation recapture amounts are recognized as ordinary income at the time of the installment sale, without regard to when payments are received.

    The recapture amounts include the following:

    – Accelerated depreciation;

    – Corporate preference amounts relating to straight-line depreciation on buildings; and

    – Rehabilitation credit basis adjustments.

- *Dealers* in personal property cannot use the installment method;

- Interest is charged on the installment sales' deferred tax for *non-dealer* real property used in a trade or business or held as rental property. This provision applies only if the real property's sales price is more than $150,000, and the deferred payments' face amount in any taxable year exceeds $5 million; and

- If any non-dealer real property installment receivable is pledged as security for a debt, the amount of debt secured is treated as a payment of the installment receivable.

- All non-dealer property sales greater than $150,000 reported on an installment basis are subject to the provisions discussed above.

Under §453(h) the distribution of installment obligations to the shareholders in a complete liquidation under §331 will not trigger immediate gain recognition by the shareholders. This is true if the installment obligations were acquired by the corporation from a sale or exchange during the twelve-month period beginning on the date a plan of complete liquidation is adopted and if the liquidation is completed during the twelve-month period.

For this rule to apply to a sale of inventory, the sale or exchange must fall under the bulk sale rules (i.e., the sale by the corporation of inventory must be to one person in one transaction and involve substantially all the property attributable to the trade or business of the corporation).

Other special provisions of §453(h) should also be considered if it is to be relied upon in a transaction.

Taxable Asset Transactions

Section 1060 – Allocation of Purchase Price

Sections 331 and 336 focus on gain or loss recognition by shareholders and their corporation, respectively, when a business is sold by the shareholders (after distribution) or directly by the corporation in a taxable asset transaction. However, another important consideration in a taxable asset transaction is how the purchase price is *allocated* to individual assets. As explained below, this allocation determines the gain or loss recognized by the seller (corporation or shareholders). Section 1060 also dictates the purchaser's allocated basis in the assets.

Allocation of Purchase Price to Individual Assets Prior to Tax Reform Act (TRA) of 1986

Prior to the Tax Reform Act (TRA) of 1986, the seller and buyer of a corporate business were typically at odds in allocating the sales price to individual assets:

- The *seller* would attempt to allocate as much of the sales price as possible to non-amortizable assets (goodwill, going concern value, etc.). This reduces the amount allocable to assets that could trigger recapture income, such as machinery and equipment.

- Alternatively, the *buyer* would attempt to allocate a large portion of the purchase price to assets such as inventory and depreciable and amortizable assets to maximize the available tax deductions. Since goodwill and going concern value did not generate tax deductions [prior to passage of the Revenue Reconciliation Act (RRA) of 1993], it was in the buyer's interest to allocate as little as possible to such assets.

"Residual" or "Gap" Method

The buyer and the seller had flexibility in the method used to allocate the purchase price. One method of allocation was the "residual" or "gap" method. Under this method the purchase price was first allocated to identifiable assets in accordance with fair market values. The excess (or residual) of the purchase price (if any) over the identified fair market value of the assets was assigned to goodwill, going concern value, or both (see Chapter 4, "Taxable Stock Transactions," regarding amortization of those items).

"Second Tier" Allocation

Also, when a taxpayer purchased a business and the apparent aggregate fair market value of the identified assets was less than the purchase price, the position was sometimes taken that the excess purchase price (or premium) could be reallocated among the identified tangible and intangible assets in proportion to their relative fair market values. This "second tier" allocation was undertaken to limit the amount otherwise allocable to goodwill and going concern value (which was not amortizable prior to the Revenue Reconciliation Act of 1993).

Adviser's Guide to Tax Consequences of the Purchase and Sale of a Business

Effect of Preferential Capital Gains Tax Treatment

In removing the preferential tax rate treatment of capital gains, Congress undermined the adverse tax positions in which the buyer and seller typically found themselves. Although a capital gains tax benefit for individual taxpayers was later reinstated, the divergent economic interests of the parties to a transaction was less effective in insuring that some realistic value was assigned to goodwill and going concern value. (**Note**: Prior to the Revenue Reconciliation Act of 1993, the buyer wanted as little as possible assigned to goodwill, since goodwill was not amortizable.)

Section 1060's Rules

In recognition of this effect, and to increase the likelihood that sellers and buyers will make consistent and economically realistic allocations, §1060 was enacted. It provides guidelines for the *allocation of the purchase price for taxable transfers of assets constituting a trade or business*. The rules will affect *both* the *buyer's basis* in the assets *and* the *seller's gain or loss* on the sale.

In the case of an "applicable asset acquisition" (defined below), §1060 requires the seller and the purchaser to allocate the consideration paid or received in a stipulated fashion. Specifically, Reg. §1.1060-1 provides special allocation rules for such asset acquisitions that follow the allocation rules of §338(b)(5).

Section 338(b)(5) (and the regulations thereunder), relate to the allocation of purchase price among the assets of an acquired corporation when a "deemed" asset purchase election under §338 is made. Broadly speaking, a §338 election allows a stock purchase to be treated as a purchase of the underlying assets. The §1060 regulations refer to the §338 regulations in addressing many of the relevant issues, indicating that similar procedures are to be followed in the event of an actual purchase of assets (under §1060) or a deemed purchase of assets (under §338). Section 338 is discussed further in Chapter 5, "Carryover of Tax Attributes."

Under §1060, the seller and purchaser must allocate the consideration under the "residual method," as outlined in Reg. §§1.338-6 and 1.338-7. This is necessary to determine, respectively, the sales price and tax basis of each asset involved in the transaction. The specifics of the residual method of allocation will be discussed shortly. But first, it's important to remember that for §1060 to apply, there must be an "applicable asset acquisition." Such an acquisition is defined to generally be:

1. Any transfer, whether direct or indirect, of a group of assets if the assets transferred constitute a trade or business in the hands of either the seller or the purchaser; and

2. The purchaser's basis in the transferred assets is determined wholly by reference to the purchaser's consideration.

A taxable purchase of the assets of an ongoing business is the most common example of an applicable asset acquisition.

An example that follows illustrates the "residual method" of allocation in such an acquisition. However, a relevant question is whether a group of assets constitute a "trade of business" for §1060 to apply in the first place. The regulations indicate that a group of assets constitutes a trade or business if:

- The use of such assets would constitute an active trade or business under §355 (dealing with tax-free spin-offs); or

- Its character is such that "goodwill" or "going concern value" could under any circumstances attach to the assets transferred in the transaction.

The §355 regulations provide some limited guidance as to what constitutes a trade or business for purposes of this code section. The other possibility is that the asset transfer involves the transfer of *goodwill or going concern value.* The §1060 regulations provide a definition of these concepts.

Goodwill is defined as the value of a trade or business attributable to the expectancy of continued customer patronage. This expectancy may be due to the name or reputation of a trade or business or any other factor.

Going concern value is the additional value that attaches to property because of its existence as an integral part of an ongoing business activity. Going concern value includes the value attributable to the ability of a trade or business to continue functioning or generating income without interruption, even though there has been a change in ownership.

The regulations also list factors that will indicate whether goodwill or going concern value are involved in a given asset transfer.

The following example illustrates the application of these rules.

Example 2-3

S is a high-grade machine shop that manufactures microwave connectors in limited quantities. It is a successful company with a reputation within the industry and among its customers for manufacturing unique, high quality products. Its tangible assets consist primarily of ordinary machinery for working metal and plating. It has no secret formulas or patented drawings of value. P is a company that designs, manufactures, and markets electronic components. It wants to establish an immediate presence in the microwave industry, an area in which it previously has not been engaged. P is acquiring assets of a number of smaller companies and hopes that these assets will collectively allow it to offer a broad product mix. P acquires the assets of S in order to augment its product mix and to promote its presence in the microwave industry.

> P will not use the assets acquired from S to manufacture microwave connectors. However, the assets transferred are assets that constitute a trade or business in the hands of the seller. Therefore, P's purchase of S's assets is an applicable asset acquisition, subject to the rules of §1060. The fact that P will not use the assets acquired from S to continue the business of S does not affect this conclusion.

Allocation of Sales/Purchase Price

As mentioned previously, for purposes of determining the seller's amount realized for each of the assets sold, the seller is to allocate consideration to all the assets sold by using the residual method under Reg. §§1.338-6 and 1.338-7. For purposes of determining the purchaser's basis in each of the assets, the purchaser also allocates consideration to all the assets purchased by using the residual method under Reg. §§1.338-6 and 1.338-7. This involves allocating the purchase price to various asset classes, as follows.

Class I assets are cash and general deposit accounts (including savings and checking accounts) other than certificates of deposit held in banks, savings and loan associations, and other depository institutions.

Class II assets are actively traded personal property and also include certificates of deposit and foreign currency even if not actively traded personal property. Class II assets include U.S. government securities and publicly traded stock.

Class III assets are assets that the taxpayer marks to market at least annually for federal income tax purposes and debt instruments (including accounts receivable). However, Class III assets do not include:

- Certain related party debt instruments;
- Certain contingent debt instruments; and
- Convertible debt instruments

Class IV assets are stock in trade of the taxpayer or other property of a kind that would properly be included in the inventory of taxpayer if on hand at the close of the taxable year, or property held by the taxpayer primarily for sale to customers in the ordinary course of its trade or business.

Class V assets are all assets other than Class I, II, III, IV, VI, and VII assets.

Class VI assets are all §197 intangibles, except goodwill and going concern value.

Class VII assets are goodwill and going concern value.

After assets in the various asset classes are identified, a prescribed purchase price allocation procedure is mandated by the regulations.

First, the purchase price is reduced by the amount of Class I assets. The excess is then allocated:

1. Among Class II acquisition date assets of the acquired company, in proportion to the fair market values of such Class II assets at that time,

2. Then among Class III assets so held in such proportion,

3. Then among Class IV assets so held in such proportion,

4. Then among Class V assets so held in such proportion,

5. Then among Class VI assets so held in such proportion, and

6. Finally, to Class VII assets.

In the event of overlap, the regulations also provide that if an asset could be includible in more than one class, then it is included in the class with the lower or lowest class number. For example, Class III has a lower class number than Class IV.

Example 2-4 illustrates application of the allocation procedures under §1060.

> **Example 2-4**
>
> On January 1, 2001, S, a sole proprietor, sells to P, a corporation, a group of assets that constitutes a trade or business for purposes of §1060. S, who plans to retire immediately, also executes in P's favor a covenant not to compete. P pays S $3,000 in cash and assumes $1,000 in liabilities. Thus, the total consideration is $4,000.
>
> On the purchase date, P and S also execute a separate agreement that states that the fair market values of the Class II, Class III, Class V, and Class VI assets S sold to P are as follows:
>
> | Asset Class | Asset | Fair Market Value |
> |:---:|:---|:---:|
> | II | Actively traded securities | $500 |
> | III | Accounts Receivable | $200 |
> | V | Furniture and fixtures | $800 |
> | | Building | $800 |
> | | Land | $200 |
> | | Equipment | $400 |
> | VI | Covenant not to compete | $900 |
>
> P and S each allocate the consideration in the transaction among the assets transferred in accordance with the agreed upon fair market values of the assets, so that $500 is allocated to Class II assets, $200 is allocated to the Class III assets, $2,200 is allocated to Class V assets, $900 is allocated to Class VI assets, and $200 ($4,000 total consideration less $3,800 allocated to assets in Classes II, III, V, and VI) is allocated to the Class VII assets (goodwill and going concern value).
>
> Therefore, the final allocation is as follows:
>
> | Asset Class | Asset | Fair Market Value |
> |:---:|:---|:---:|
> | I | None | N/A |
> | II | Actively traded securities | $500 |
> | III | Accounts receivable | $200 |
> | IV | None | N/A |
> | V | Furniture and fixtures | $800 |
> | | Building | $800 |
> | | Land | $200 |
> | | Equipment | $400 |
> | VI | Covenant not to compete | $900 |
> | VII | Goodwill/going concern | $200 |

Effect of a Written Agreement Between the Parties

If the seller and purchaser agree in writing as to the allocation of the purchase price to the assets transferred, such agreement is generally binding on them.

While the IRS is free to challenge the allocations or values included in an allocation agreement, taxpayers generally can only refute a written allocation or valuation under the standards set forth in *Danielson*, 378 F2d 771 (3d Cir.), cert. denied, 389 U.S. 858 (1967). This means that a taxpayer wishing to challenge the tax consequences of a written agreement must offer proof that the agreement involved a mistake, undue influence, fraud, or duress.

Subsequent Adjustment

The purchase price originally stated in the sales agreement may subsequently change due to any number of reasons — to include the existence of contingent consideration that is recognized in later years, a contingent liability, or an IRS adjustment. For example, in examining a taxpayer's return, the IRS, in determining the fair market values of the assets transferred, may disregard the parties' agreement.

In the preceding example, assume that the IRS correctly determines that the fair market value of the covenant not to compete was $500. Since the allocation of consideration among Class II, III, V, and VI assets results in allocation up to the fair market value limitation, the $600 unallocated consideration resulting from the IRS' re-determination of the value of the covenant not to compete is allocated to Class VII assets (goodwill and going concern value).

Regulation §§1.338-6 and 1.338-7 provide specific rules that are to be followed for the re-allocation of basis to purchased assets in the event there is a subsequent adjustment to the original purchase price.

Reporting Requirements

The seller and the purchaser in an applicable asset acquisition each must report information concerning the amount of consideration in the transaction and its allocation among the assets transferred. They also must report information concerning subsequent adjustments to consideration. See Form 8594, *Asset Acquisition Statement (Under Section 1060)* for an example of the information required. The reporting requirements are discussed further later in the book.

Acquisition Related Costs

The regulations provide that the seller and purchaser are to adjust the amount allocated to an individual asset to take into account the specific identifiable costs incurred in transferring that asset. Examples are real estate transfer costs or security interest perfection costs. Costs so allocated increase or decrease the total consideration that is allocated under §1060. However, no adjustment is to be made to the amount allocated to an individual asset for general costs associated with the acquisition as a whole (or with groups of assets). Examples of these latter types of costs are non-specific appraisal fees or accounting fees. These latter amounts are taken into account only indirectly through their effect on the total consideration to be allocated. There is a further discussion of acquisition costs later in the book.

Summary

Acquisitions can involve either a transfer of assets or stock. In this chapter the consequences of an asset sale were discussed. An asset sale has tax and non-tax advantages and disadvantages.

Asset sales can involve the use of the installment sales method. While the installment method defers the tax liability of the seller, it also results in the seller not having access to all of the proceeds. Also, the installment method can trigger immediate tax liability from recapture income in the year of sale, even if no cash is received.

Section 1060 contains rules for the allocation of sales price to purchased assets constituting a trade or business and it affects both buyer and seller. It also contains reporting requirements that must be followed by the buyer and seller. These reporting requirements make it easier for the IRS to monitor purchase-price allocations.

Case Study 2-1

Case Study 2-1 — Dodger Manufacturing Corporation

Assume

Dodger Manufacturing Corporation (the Corporation) has been in the business of manufacturing super flight high intensity baseballs for four years, experiencing consistent profits and rapid growth. It is a closely held corporation (i.e., its stock is not publicly traded).

All three stockholders are active in the business: Maury Koufax, President; Wes Drysdale, Vice President; and Tom Podres, Secretary Treasurer. When the Corporation was formed, the stockholders invested $100,000 and received shares of common stock ($100 par value) as follows:

Koufax	500 shares	$ 50,000
Drysdale	300 shares	30,000
Podres	200 shares	20,000
Total	1,000 shares	$100,000

The officers/stockholders want to retire from the business. Willie Marichal is contemplating the purchase of Dodger Manufacturing Corporation. Marichal is in the business of manufacturing cork filled natural wood baseball bats and is looking to diversify and integrate his business.

Willie Marichal and Maury Koufax have agreed on the fair market value of each asset presently owned by Dodger.

Koufax is willing to sell either the assets for $510,000 or the stock of Dodger Manufacturing Corporation for $360,000. The $360,000 offer is based on the fair market value of the stockholders' equity on the statement of financial position shown below.

Dodger Manufacturing Corporation Statement of Financial Position

Assets	Basis per Tax Books	Fair Market Value
Cash	$ 10,000	$ 10,000
Accounts Receivable	30,000	30,000
Inventory	100,000	110,000
Equipment (net of $20,000 straight-line depreciation)	20,000	35,000
Plant and Property ($40,000 of straight-line depreciation)	180,000	250,000
Supplies	NONE	5,000
Prepaid Insurance	5,000	5,000
Goodwill	NONE	65,000
Total Assets	$345,000	$510,000

Liabilities and Stockholders' Equity

Current liabilities	$ 50,000	$ 50,000
Mortgage	100,000	100,000
Total Liabilities	$150,000	$150,000

Stockholders' equity

Capital stock	$100,000	
Retained earnings	95,000	
Total stockholders' equity	195,000	360,000
Total liabilities and stockholders' equity	$345,000	$510,000

Case Study 2-1 — Questions & Answers

Question 1. Assume that Marichal will not accept a stock purchase. He wants to purchase the corporate assets. What would be the tax consequence if the corporation sells its assets for $510,000 (the liabilities will not be assumed)? At this point, ignore the impact of the subsequent liquidation of the corporation.

Assumptions

- The sale is expected to take place on January 2, 19X7.

- Investment tax credit recapture on the equipment is zero.

- Assume a marginal tax rate of 35% (ignore the impact of the graduated corporate tax rates).

Answer 1. The computation of the corporate gain on the sale of assets is outlined on the following schedule.

Note that in accordance with §1060, the assets are divided into the appropriate classes and the sales price allocated consecutively to the classes to the extent of, but not in excess of, fair market value.

Sale of Corporate Assets Section 1060 Allocation Computation of Taxable Income and Income Tax Payable

					Gain or Loss	
Assets	**Class***	**Basis Per Tax Books**	**Fair Market Value**	**Ordinary Income Assets**	**Section 1231 Assets**	**Capital Gain**
Cash	I	$ 10,000	$ 10,000	$ –	$ –	$ –
Accounts Receivable	III	30,000	30,000	–	–	–
Inventory	IV	100,000	110,000	10,000	–	–
Equipment (net of $20,000 straight-line depreciation)	V	20,000	35,000	15,000	–	–
Plant and Property (net of $40,000 of straight-line depreciation)	V	180,000	250,000	8,000***	62,000	–
Supplies	V	NONE	5,000	5,000*	–	–
Prepaid Insurance	V	5,000	5,000	–	–	–
Goodwill	VII	NONE	65,000	–	–	65,000**
Total Assets		$345,000	$510,000			
Total gain				$38,000	$ 62,000	$ 65,000
Corporate tax					$ 57,750	

* Note there are no Class II or Class VI assets in this example.

** Note that because the purchase price exceeds the fair market value of the identified assets, the excess of $65,000 is allocable to goodwill.

*** Under Section 291(a)(1): $40,000 Accum. Depreciation
  × .2
  $ 8,000

Although the stockholders have a basis of $100,000 in their stock, the Corporation's basis in its assets is $345,000.

Thus, if the Corporation sells the assets for $510,000, without the buyer assuming the liabilities, it would have the following:

- A capital gain of $65,000,

- §1231 gain of $62,000, and

- Ordinary income of $38,000.

Since corporate ordinary income and capital gains are taxed at the same tax rate (assume a marginal rate of 35%), the tax on the $165,000 of total tax gain would be $57,750.

Question 2. As in Question 1, assume that Marichal wants assets, not stock. What would be the tax effect to the stockholders if the corporation instead adopted a plan of liquidation, distributed the assets to the stockholders, and the stockholders sold the assets in their individual capacities? For simplicity of calculation, assume a 20% capital gains tax rate for the shareholders.

Answer 2. Pursuant to §336, Dodger Manufacturing Corporation would recognize income on the liquidation distributions as if the property were sold at its fair market value. The gain to the Corporation on the property distributions would be equal to the gain calculated in Question 1 (as if the Corporation sold its assets).

The stockholders would treat the receipt of the net assets as full payment in exchange for their stock, and realize a capital gain computed as follows:

Fair market value of assets	$ 510,000
Less: Tax liability from corporate distribution	(57,750)
Other liabilities assumed	(150,000)
Net Value	$ 302,250
Less basis of stockholders' stock	(100,000)
Long-term gain to stockholders	$ 202,250
Tax to stockholders at 20% rate	$ 40,450

Note: The above analysis assumes the sale to Marichal takes place immediately after the corporate distribution of assets. Since the basis of the assets is stepped-up to fair market value in the hands of the stockholders, there would be no gain or loss on the immediate sale of the assets to Marichal.

Question 3. What factors would suggest that an asset purchase would be preferable to Marichal?

Answer 3. An asset purchase appears desirable from Marichal's perspective for the following reasons:

- He can obtain the assets of Dodger at a stepped-up basis (since their value exceeds their historical tax basis). This will increase depreciation and amortization deductions.

- He will avoid assuming any undisclosed liabilities of Dodger.

- In this case there is no indication of any desirable tax attributes (e.g., NOLs) that would be made unavailable in an asset purchase.

Question 4. Would installment sale treatment be available for the asset sale?

Answer 4. Yes, based on the facts, the corporation could sell the assets to Marichal on the installment basis, taking back a note for all or a portion of the proceeds. This note would be distributed to the shareholders in liquidation. This would not trigger immediate gain recognition to the shareholders provided the requirements of §453(h) were satisfied.

Alternatively, the corporation could distribute all its assets in complete liquidation and allow the shareholders to sell the assets to Marichal on the installment basis.

Taxable Asset Transactions

IRS Form 8594

Taxable Asset Transactions

Form 8594
(Rev. October 2002)
Department of the Treasury
Internal Revenue Service

Asset Acquisition Statement Under Section 1060

▶ Attach to your income tax return. ▶ See separate instructions.

OMB No. 1545-1021

Attachment Sequence No. **61**

Name as shown on return

Identifying number as shown on return

Check the box that identifies you:
☐ Purchaser   ☐ Seller

Part I General Information

1 Name of other party to the transaction

Other party's identifying number

Address (number, street, and room or suite no.)

City or town, state, and ZIP code

2 Date of sale

3 Total sales price (consideration)

Part II Assets Transferred—All filers of an original statement must complete.

4 Assets	Aggregate fair market value (actual amount for Class I)	Allocation of sales price
Class I	$	$
Class II	$	$
Class III	$	$
Class IV	$	$
Class V	$	$
Class VI and VII	$	$
Total	$	$

5 Did the purchaser and seller provide for an allocation of the sales price in the sales contract or in another written document signed by both parties? . . . . ☐ Yes ☐ No

If "Yes," are the aggregate fair market values (FMV) listed for each of asset Classes I, II, III, IV, V, VI, and VII the amounts agreed upon in your sales contract or in a separate written document? . . . . . . ☐ Yes ☐ No

6 In the purchase of the group of assets (or stock), did the purchaser also purchase a license or a covenant not to compete, or enter into a lease agreement, employment contract, management contract, or similar arrangement with the seller (or managers, directors, owners, or employees of the seller)? . . . . . ☐ Yes ☐ No

If "Yes," attach a schedule that specifies **(a)** the type of agreement and **(b)** the maximum amount of consideration (not including interest) paid or to be paid under the agreement. See instructions.

For Paperwork Reduction Act Notice, see separate instructions.   Cat. No. 63768Z   Form **8594** (Rev. 10-2002)

Adviser's Guide to Tax Consequences of the Purchase and Sale of a Business

Form 8594 (Rev. 10-2002) Page **2**

Part III **Supplemental Statement**—Complete only if amending an original statement or previously filed supplemental statement because of an increase or decrease in consideration.

7 Tax year and tax return form number with which the original Form 8594 and any supplemental statements were filed.

8 Assets	Allocation of sales price as previously reported	Increase or (decrease)	Redetermined allocation of sales price
Class I	$	$	$
Class II	$	$	$
Class III	$	$	$
Class IV	$	$	$
Class V	$	$	$
Class VI and VII	$	$	$
Total	$		$

9 Reason(s) for increase or decrease. Attach additional sheets if more space is needed.

Form **8594** (Rev. 10-2002)

Taxable Asset Transactions

Instructions for Form 8594
(Rev. October 2002)
Asset Acquisition Statement Under Section 1060

Department of the Treasury
Internal Revenue Service

Section references are to the Internal Revenue Code unless otherwise noted.

General Instructions

Changes To Note
New regulations have made significant changes to the rules applicable under section 1060. The regulations are effective for allocations of assets acquired or deemed acquired after March 15, 2001. Among the most important changes are the addition of new Class III, which is applicable to mark-to-market assets, certain debt instruments, and new Class IV, which is applicable to inventory.

Purpose of Form
Both the seller and purchaser of a group of assets that makes up a trade or business must use Form 8594 to report such a sale if goodwill or going concern value attaches, or could attach, to such assets and if the purchaser's basis in the assets is determined only by the amount paid for the assets.

Form 8594 must also be filed if the purchaser or seller is amending an original or a previously filed supplemental Form 8594 because of an increase or decrease in the purchaser's cost of the assets or the amount realized by the seller.

Who Must File
Subject to the exceptions noted below, both purchaser and seller of the assets must file Form 8594 and attach it to their income tax returns (Forms 1040, 1041, 1065, 1120, 1120S, etc.) when there is a transfer of a group of assets that make up a trade or business (defined below) and the purchaser's basis in such assets is determined wholly by the amount paid for the assets. This applies whether the group of assets constitutes a trade or business in the hands of the seller, the purchaser, or both.

If the purchaser or seller is a controlled foreign corporation (CFC), each U.S. shareholder should attach Form 8594 to its Form 5471.

Exceptions. You are **not** required to file Form 8594 if any of the following apply:
- A group of assets that makes up a trade or business is exchanged for like-kind property in a transaction to which section 1031 applies. If section 1031 does not apply to all the assets transferred, however, Form 8594 is required for the part of the group of assets to which section 1031 does not apply. For information about such a transaction, see Regulations sections 1.1031(j)-1(b) and 1.1060-1(b)(8).
- A partnership interest is transferred. See Temporary Regulations section 1.755-2T for special reporting requirements.

When To File
Generally, attach Form 8594 to your income tax return for the year in which the sale date occurred.

If the amount allocated to any asset is increased or decreased after the year in which the sale occurs, the seller and/or purchaser (whoever is affected) must complete Parts I and III of Form 8594 and attach the form to the income tax return for the year in which the increase or decrease is taken into account.

Penalty
If you fail to file a correct Form 8594 by the due date of your return and you cannot show reasonable cause, you may be subject to a penalty. See sections 6721 through 6724.

Definitions
Trade or business. A group of assets makes up a trade or business if goodwill or going concern value could under any circumstances attach to such assets. A group of assets can also qualify as a trade or business if it qualifies as an active trade or business under section 355 (relating to distributions of stock in controlled corporations.

Factors to consider in determining whether goodwill or going concern value could attach include **(a)** the presence of any section 197 or other intangible assets (but the transfer of such an asset in the absence of other assets will not be a trade or business), **(b)** any excess of the total paid for the assets over the aggregate book value of the assets (other than goodwill or going concern value) as shown in the purchaser's financial accounting books and records, or **(c)** a license, a lease agreement, a covenant not to compete, a management contract, an employment contract, or other similar agreements between purchaser and seller (or managers, directors, owners, or employees of the seller).

Consideration. The purchaser's consideration is the cost of the assets. The purchaser's consideration is the amount realized.

Fair market value. Fair market value is the gross fair market value unreduced by mortgages, liens, pledges, or other liabilities. However, for determining the seller's gain or loss, generally, the fair market value of any property is not less than any nonrecourse debt to which the property is subject.

Classes of assets. The following definitions are the classifications effective for deemed or actual asset acquisitions on or after March 16, 2001.

Class I assets are cash and general deposit accounts (including savings and checking accounts) other than certificates of deposit held in banks, savings and loan associations, and other depository institutions.

Class II assets are actively traded personal property within the meaning of section 1092(d)(1) and Regulations section 1.1092(d)-1 (determined without regard to section 1092(d)(3)). In addition, Class II assets include certificates of deposit and foreign currency even if they are not actively traded personal property. Class II assets do not include stock of target affiliates, whether or not actively traded, other than actively traded stock described in section 1504(a)(4). Examples of Class II assets include U.S. government securities and publicly traded stock.

Cat. No. 29292S

2-29

Adviser's Guide to Tax Consequences of the Purchase and Sale of a Business

Class III assets are assets that the taxpayer marks-to-market at least annually for Federal income tax purposes and debt instruments (including accounts receivable). However, Class III assets do not include **(a)** debt instruments issued by persons related at the beginning of the day following the acquisition date to the target under section 267(b) or 707; **(b)** contingent debt instruments subject to Regulations sections 1.1275-4 and 1.483-4, or section 988, unless the instrument is subject to the noncontingent bond method of Regulations section 1.1275-4(b) or is described in Regulations section 1.988-2(b)(2)(i)(B)(2); and **(c)** debt instruments convertible into the stock of the issuer or other property.

Class IV assets are stock in trade of the taxpayer or other property of a kind that would properly be included in the inventory of the taxpayer if on hand at the close of the taxable year, or property held by the taxpayer primarily for sale to customers in the ordinary course of its trade or business.

Class V assets are all assets other than Class I, II, III, IV, VI and VII assets.

Class VI assets are all section 197 intangibles (as defined in section 197) except goodwill and going concern value. Section 197 intangibles include:
- Workforce in place;
- Business books and records, operating systems, or any other information base, process, design, pattern, know-how, formula, or similar item;
- Any customer-based intangible;
- Any supplier-based intangible;
- Any license, permit, or other right granted by a government unit;
- Any covenant not to compete entered into in connection with the acquisition of an interest in a trade or a business; and
- Any franchise (other than a sports franchise), trademark, or trade name.

However, the term "section 197 intangible" does not include any of the following:
- An interest in a corporation, partnership, trust, or estate;
- Interests under certain financial contracts;
- Interests in land;
- Certain computer software;
- Certain separately acquired interests in films, sound recordings, video tapes, books, or other similar property;
- Interests under leases of tangible property;
- Certain separately acquired rights to receive tangible property or services;
- Certain separately acquired interests in patents or copyrights;
- Interests under indebtedness;
- Professional sports franchises; and
- Certain transactions costs.

See section 197(e) for further information.

Class VII assets are goodwill and going concern value (whether or not the goodwill or going concern value qualifies as a section 197 intangible).

Allocation of consideration. An allocation of the purchase price must be made to determine the purchaser's basis in each acquired asset and the seller's gain or loss on the transfer of each asset. Use the residual method for the allocation of the sales price among the amortizable section 197 intangibles and other assets transferred. See Regulations section 1.1060-1(c). The amount allocated to an asset, other than a Class VII asset, cannot exceed its fair market value on the purchase date. The amount you can allocate to an asset also is subject to any applicable limits under the Internal Revenue Code or general principals of tax law. For example, see section 1056 for the basis limitation for player contracts transferred in connection with the sale of a franchise.

Consideration should be allocated as follows: **(a)** reduce the consideration by the amount of Class I assets transferred, **(b)** allocate the remaining consideration to Class II assets in proportion to their fair market values on the purchase date, **(c)** allocate to Class III assets in proportion to their fair market values on the purchase date, **(d)** allocate to Class IV assets in proportion to their fair market values on the purchase date, **(e)** allocate to Class V assets in proportion to their fair market values on the purchase date, **(f)** allocate to Class VI assets in proportion to their fair market values on the purchase date, and **(g)** allocate to Class VII assets. If an asset in one of the classifications described above can be included in more than one class, choose the lower numbered class (e.g., if an asset could be included in Class III or IV, choose Class III).

Reallocation after an increase or decrease in consideration. If an increase or decrease in consideration that must be taken into account to redetermine the seller's amount realized on the sale, or the purchaser's cost basis in the assets, occurs after the purchase date, the seller and/or purchaser must allocate the increase or decrease among the assets. If the increase or decrease occurs in the same tax year as the purchase date, consider the increase or decrease to have occurred on the purchase date. If the increase or decrease occurs after the tax year of the purchase date, consider it in the tax year in which it occurs.

For an increase or decrease related to a patent, copyright, etc., see **Specific Allocation** on page 3.

Allocation of increase. Allocate an increase in consideration as described under **Allocation of consideration**. If an asset has been disposed of, depreciated, amortized, or depleted by the purchaser before the increase occurs, any amount allocated to that asset by the purchaser must be properly taken into account under principles of tax law applicable when part of the cost of an asset (not previously reflected in its basis) is paid after the asset has been disposed of, depreciated, amortized, or depleted.

Allocation of decrease. Allocate a decrease in consideration as follows: **(a)** reduce the amount previously allocated to Class VII assets, **(b)** reduce the amount previously allocated to Class VI assets in proportion to their fair market values on the purchase date, **(c)** reduce the amount previously allocated to Class V assets in proportion to their fair market values on the purchase date, **(d)** reduce the amount previously allocated to Class IV assets in proportion to their fair market values on the purchase date, **(e)** reduce the amount previously allocated to Class III assets in proportion to their fair market values on the purchase date, and **(f)** reduce the amount previously allocated to Class II assets in proportion to their fair market values on the purchase date.

You cannot decrease the amount allocated to an asset below zero. If an asset has a basis of zero at the time the decrease is taken into account because it has been disposed of, depreciated, amortized, or depleted by the purchaser under section 1060, the decrease in consideration allocable to such asset must be properly taken into account under the principles of tax law applicable when the cost of an asset (previously reflected in basis) is reduced after the asset has been disposed of, depreciated, amortized, or depleted. An asset is considered to have been disposed of to the extent the decrease allocated to it would reduce its basis below zero.

Patents, copyrights, and similar property. You must make a specific allocation (defined below) if an increase or decrease in consideration is the result of a contingency that directly relates to income produced by a particular intangible asset, such as a patent, a secret process, or a copyright, and the increase or decrease is related only to such asset and not to other assets. If the specific allocation rule does not apply, make an allocation of any increase or decrease as you would for any other assets as described under **Allocation of increase** and **Allocation of decrease.**

Specific allocation. Limited to the fair market value of the asset, any increase or decrease in consideration is allocated first specifically to the patent, copyright, or similar property to which the increase or decrease relates, and then to the other assets in the order described under **Allocation of increase** and **Allocation of decrease.** For purposes of applying the fair market value limit to the patent, copyright, or similar property, the fair market value of such asset is redetermined when the increase or decrease is taken into account by considering only the reasons for the increase or decrease. The fair market values of the other assets are not redetermined.

Specific Instructions

For an original statement, complete Parts I and II. For a Supplemental Statement, complete Part I and III.

Enter your name and taxpayer identification number (TIN) at the top of the form. Then check the box for purchaser or seller.

Part I—General Information

Line 1. Enter the name, address, and TIN of the other party to the transaction (purchaser or seller). You are required to enter the TIN of the other party. If the other party is an individual or sole proprietor, enter the social security number. If the other party is a corporation, partnership, or other entity, enter the employer identification number.

Line 2. Enter the date on which the sale of the assets occurred.

Line 3. Enter the total consideration transferred for the assets.

Part II—Assets Transferred

Line 4. For a particular class of assets, enter the total fair market value of all the assets in the class and the total allocation of the sales price. For Classes VI and XII, enter the total fair market value of Class VI and Class VII combined, and the total portion of the sales price allocated to Class VI and Class VII combined.

Line 6. This line must be completed by the purchaser and the seller. To determine the maximum consideration to be paid, assume that any contingencies specified in the agreement are met and that the consideration paid is the highest amount possible. If you cannot determine the maximum consideration, state how the consideration will be computed and the payment period.

Part III—Supplemental Statement

Complete Part III and file a new Form 8594 for each year that an increase or decrease in consideration occurs. Give the reason(s) for the increase or decrease in allocation. Also, enter the tax year(s) and form number with which the original and any supplemental statements were filed. For example, enter "2001 Form 1040".

Paperwork Reduction Act Notice. We ask for the information on this form to carry out the Internal Revenue laws of the United States. You are required to give us the information. We need it to ensure that you are complying with these laws and to allow us to figure and collect the right amount of tax.

You are not required to provide the information requested on a form that is subject to the Paperwork Reduction Act unless the form displays a valid OMB control number. Books or records relating to a form or its instructions must be retained as long as their contents may become material in the administration of any Internal Revenue law. Generally, tax returns and return information are confidential, as required by section 6103.

The time needed to complete and file this tax form will vary depending on individual circumstances. The estimated average time is:

Recordkeeping	11 hr.
Learning about the law or the form	2 hr., 34 min.
Preparing and sending the form to the IRS	2 hr., 52 min.

If you have comments concerning the accuracy of these time estimates or suggestions for making this form simpler, we would be happy to hear from you. You can write to the IRS at the address listed in the instructions for the tax return with which this form is filed.

Chapter 3

Purchases Involving Intangible Assets

Objective

This chapter will explain the tax considerations related to intangible assets.

Introduction

In Chapter 2, "Taxable Asset Transactions," reference was made to the identification and valuation of intangible assets. Perhaps the most common intangible assets are goodwill and going concern value. These assets can be defined as follows:

- **Goodwill** is the value inherent in the favorable consideration of customers arising from an established and well-known business enterprise.

- **Going concern value** is the enhanced asset value inherent in a business that is already in operation (i.e., the forbearance of startup costs).

Most acquisitions involve the allocation of a portion of the purchase price to goodwill and/or going concern value.

Background

Until 1993, from the buyer's standpoint amounts allocated to such assets were not amortizable and yielded no tax benefit through amortization deductions.

As a result, for many years buyers sought to identify and value intangible assets that were separable from goodwill and going-concern value. This would yield tax deductions to the buyer. If such intangibles could be shown to have a determinable life that could be measured with reasonable accuracy, then there was support for deducting the amortization of the asset.

Alternatively, if a fixed life could not be reasonably determined for an asset, it was possible to obtain a tax benefit through an abandonment deduction (if and when the identified asset was abandoned).

We will first discuss some assets whose identification, valuation, and life (to allow amortization) was commonplace under prior law. We will then consider how the law has changed and how these procedures may still be appropriate.

Separable and Valuable Intangibles – Pre-Revenue Reconciliation Act (RRA) of 1993

Under prior law, goodwill and going-concern values were not amortizable for tax purposes. Therefore, to the extent other intangible assets could be identified and valued, and an estimated life could be determined by a purchaser, such intangible assets could increase the purchaser's tax benefits.

Following is a listing of some common intangible assets that could yield tax benefits to a buyer:

- Patents
- Patent applications
- Franchises, trademarks, and trade names
- Copyrights
- Formulae, processes, and unpatented inventions
- Licenses and franchises
- Favorable leases
- Favorable contracts
- Customer lists
- Computer software
- Dealer/distributor networks
- Covenants not to compete.

Identification of such assets was also important to the seller. Remember that §1060 requires an asset-by-asset allocation of sales price. The nature of the gain or loss (albeit not the total amount of gain or loss) recognized by the seller will depend on the allocation of the sales price to the individual assets and the nature of these assets (e.g., §1231, 1245, 1250 or capital).

Purchases Involving Intangible Assets

To the extent that the above intangible assets are not identified, the excess purchase price (if any) is allocated to goodwill or going concern value. Such assets generate capital gain to the seller. For example, if §1231type assets are identified, a portion of the gain would be converted from capital to §1231 gain.

Such considerations were of greater importance to individuals after their capital gain/ordinary income tax differential was reinstated. Accordingly, sellers were concerned about the impact on their tax position if such assets were identified in the purchase agreement.

Of course, tax consequences aside, to the extent that the seller can identify intangible assets, he or she might obtain a higher sales price that reflects the value of these assets.

During the 1980s and 1990s, there were a number of court cases involving the amortization of intangible assets. The most important of these cases was the decision in *Newark Morning Ledger* (93-1, USTC, para.50,228). This case involved a taxpayer's amortization of purchase price allocated to customer lists. These customer lists were acquired as part of the purchase of a newspaper organization. The IRS had argued the "customer lists" were inseparable from goodwill and therefore could not be amortized by the taxpayer. The U.S. Court of Appeals for the Third Circuit agreed with the IRS and disallowed the deduction claimed by the taxpayer.

However, the taxpayer appealed to the U.S. Supreme Court, which rejected the IRS argument that as a matter of law taxpayers could not amortize certain intangibles. Instead, the Court held that taxpayers were entitled to amortization of intangibles, provided they could substantiate a definitive useful life and ascertain the value of the intangibles. Such amortization was permissible, in the Court's opinion, regardless of how much the asset appeared to reflect the expectancy of continued patronage (i.e., goodwill, which was not amortizable for tax purposes).

While the Supreme Court upheld such amortization in principle, it also indicated that taxpayers would, as a practical matter, have a difficult time sustaining the amortization deduction. This was due to the enormous burden of proof taxpayers had (e.g., producing appropriate documentation to support the limited life and/or value of the intangible).

Revenue Reconciliation Act of 1993 – Amortization of Intangible Assets

Congress was concerned about the level of controversy surrounding the amortization of intangibles (in terms of the time and resources being expended in disputes between the IRS and taxpayers).

This concern was not lessened by the Supreme Court decision in *Newark Morning Ledger*, which promised continuing litigation. To limit the controversy in this area, Congress provided new rules governing the amortization of what is defined as §197 assets. This reference is to intangible assets specifically listed in §197.

Section 197 assets include the following categories of intangibles:

1. Goodwill and going concern value;
2. Work force;
3. Information base;
4. Know-how;
5. Customer-based intangibles (e.g., customer base or circulation base);
6. Supplier-based intangibles (e.g., favorable supply contracts or a favorable credit rating);
7. Any license, permit, or other right granted by a governmental unit;
8. A covenant not to compete or similar arrangement;
9. Franchises;
10. Trademarks; and
11. Trade names.

Section 197 assets, which are purchased in a taxable asset acquisition (or in a stock purchase electively treated as an asset purchase under §338), will be subject to 15-year straight-line amortization to the extent of their allocated tax basis.

Some of these intangibles covered by the provisions of §197 intangibles are worthy of further comment.

Workforce

Workforce includes the composition of a workforce. This can include

- The experience, education, or training of a workforce,
- The terms and conditions of employment whether contractual or otherwise, and
- Any other value placed on employees or any of their attributes.

Purchases Involving Intangible Assets

Regulation 1.197-2 indicates that the amount paid or incurred for workforce in place includes

- Any portion of the purchase price of an acquired trade or business attributable to the existence of a highly-skilled workforce.

- An existing employment contract (or contracts), or

- A relationship with employees or consultants (including, but not limited to, any key employee contract or relationship).

Information Base

Section 197 intangibles include any information base, including a customer-related information base. An information base includes business books and records and operating systems. A customer-related information base is any information base that includes lists or other information with respect to current or prospective customers.

The amount paid for information base includes any portion of the purchase price of an acquired trade or business attributable to the intangible value of

- Technical manuals,

- Training manuals or programs,

- Data files, and

- Accounting or inventory control systems.

Information base can also include the cost of acquiring customer lists, subscription lists, insurance expirations, patient or client files, or lists of newspaper, magazine, radio, or television advertisers.

Customer-Based Intangible

Regulation 1.197-2 indicates that a customer-based intangible is any composition of market, market share, or other value resulting from the future provision of goods or services pursuant to contractual or other relationships in the ordinary course of business with customers.

The amount paid for customer-based intangibles includes any portion of the purchase price of an acquired trade or business attributable to the existence of

- A customer base,

- A circulation base,

- An undeveloped market or market growth,

- Insurance in force,

- The existence of a qualification to supply goods or services to a particular customer,

- A mortgage servicing contract,

- An investment management contract, or

- Any other relationship with customers involving the future provision of goods or services.

In addition, customer-based intangibles include the deposit base and any similar asset of a financial institution.

However, any portion of the purchase price of an acquired trade or business attributable to accounts receivable is not an amount paid or incurred for a customer-based intangible.

Supplier-Based Intangible

A supplier-based intangible is the value resulting from the future acquisition, under a contractual or other relationship with suppliers in the ordinary course of business, of goods or services that will be sold or used by the taxpayer.

The amount paid for supplier-based intangibles includes

- Any portion of the purchase price of an acquired trade or business attributable to the existence of a favorable relationship with persons providing distribution services (such as favorable shelf or display space at a retail outlet),

- The existence of a favorable credit rating, or

- The existence of favorable supply contracts.

Know-How

Section 197 intangibles include any patent, copyright, formula, process, design, pattern, know-how, format, package design, computer software or interest in a film, sound recording, video tape, book, or other similar property.

Purchases Involving Intangible Assets

Governmental License

Section 197 intangibles include any license, permit, or other right granted by a governmental unit. The regulations provide that this is true even if the right is granted for an indefinite period or is reasonably expected to be renewed for an indefinite period.

These rights can include

- A liquor license,
- A taxi-cab medallion (or license),
- An airport landing or takeoff right (sometimes referred to as a slot),
- A regulated airline route, or
- A television or radio broadcasting license.

Franchise, Trademark or Trade Name

Section 197 intangibles include any franchise, trademark, or trade name.

The term **franchise** includes any agreement that provides one of the parties to the agreement with the right to distribute, sell, or provide goods, services, or facilities, within a specified area.

The term **trademark** includes any word, name, symbol, or device, or any combination thereof, adopted and used to identify goods or services and distinguish them from those provided by others.

The term **trade name** includes any name used to identify or designate a particular trade or business or the name or title used by a person or organization engaged in a trade or business.

Excluded Assets

Certain intangible assets were specifically excluded from §197. In general, these excluded assets are to be amortized either under the provisions of existing law (e.g., interests in land) or in accordance with guidance provided by Congress (e.g., 36-month amortization for certain types of computer software).

Assets specifically excluded from §197 classification include the following:

1. Certain financial interests (e.g., an interest in a corporation, partnership, trust or estate, or in an existing futures contract or foreign currency contract);

2. Any interest in land;

3. Certain types of computer software;

4. Certain interests in films, sound recordings, videotapes, books, or other similar property;

5. Certain rights to receive tangible property or services;

6. Interests under leases and debt instruments;

7. Certain interests in patents or copyrights;

8. Any interest under an existing lease of tangible property;

9. Certain interests in existing indebtedness;

10. Sports franchises;

11. Purchased mortgage-serving rights;

12. Certain transaction costs; and

13. Certain self-created intangibles (e.g., a technological process developed by the taxpayer under an arrangement with another person, pursuant to which the taxpayer retains all rights).

Special Rules Concerning Section 197 Intangibles

Special rules also apply to the disposition of §197 intangibles. These can apply if, for example, a taxpayer disposes of a §197 asset that was acquired in a transaction and, after the transaction, the taxpayer retains other §197 assets that were acquired in the transaction.

If more than one §197 asset is acquired in an acquisition (which will likely be the case), gain is recognized on the sale or disposition of each intangible. However, loss is recognized only when the taxpayer disposes of the last of the §197 intangibles. Any loss not recognized increases the basis of the retained §197 intangibles (this is done on a proportional basis). Furthermore, covenants not to compete cannot be considered worthless for tax purposes until the disposition of the ownership entire interest to which the covenant is related.

There are also anti-churning rules (i.e., rules designed to prevent a taxpayer from converting existing goodwill or other intangible asset not allowed to be amortized into an asset that could be amortized under the law).

The rules apply to property acquired after *August 10, 1993*.

Tax Planning

Impact on Acquisition Economics

The rules for the amortization of intangibles affect the economics of asset purchases. The buyer will be able to amortize costs such as goodwill/going concern value that were not amortizable prior to the Revenue Reconciliation Act (RRA) of 1993. To the contrary, buyers will be forced to use longer amortization periods for certain assets amortizable under prior law (e.g., a covenant not to compete, now amortizable over a 15-year period rather than its term of enforcement).

Use of Independent Valuation Services

Professional valuation services are still useful. First, they can help the buyer (and the seller) identify exactly what intangibles are being transferred from seller to buyer. This can impact the economics of the transaction.

From the buyer's tax perspective there continue to be reasons why a valuation is important. First, several types of intangibles are not covered by the 15-year straight-line amortization of §197. A valuation can help establish a useful life and value to permit the amortization of such assets.

Secondly, as mentioned previously, there is a special rule with respect to abandonment losses for intangibles. Specifically, the rule for "bundled" §197 intangibles will require taxpayers to separately value §197 intangibles. This will be necessary to determine the initial relative adjusted basis for absorbing any loss subsequently recognized.

Furthermore, a separate valuation is required to see if a subsequent disposition results in a gain that must be recognized or a loss that has to be deferred under the new rules.

From the seller's tax perspective the gain recognized in an asset sale can still be different (capital gain/loss vs. §1231 gain/loss) depending on how the purchase price is allocated between intangibles (e.g., between goodwill and software). This was not changed by RRA of 1993. Therefore, sellers should still be concerned with a defensible allocation of purchase price to the assets being sold.

Regulatory Guidance

Regulations 1.97-1 and 2 (and the related proposed regulations) provide regulatory guidance on the application of §197, including those matters referred to above. These regulations deal with such issues as the amortization of assets excluded from §197, special rules for computer software, and the application of the §197 rules to partnership transactions.

Summary

This chapter contains a discussion of intangible assets that yield tax benefits. For years the IRS prevailed in asserting that any transferred intangible assets should be treated as goodwill or going concern value, neither of which yielded amortization deductions to a purchaser. Conflict between taxpayers and the IRS resulted in frequent litigation.

Congress sought to end much of the disagreement by enacting special 15-year amortization for many intangible assets now included in §197. However, certain intangible assets are excluded from §197 classification and continue to be treated either under prior law or current guidelines established by Congress (e.g., amortization of certain types of software).

For various reasons, identification and valuation of intangibles continue to be of importance.

Many intangibles, including most intangibles acquired in connection with the purchase of a business, are to be amortized over 15 years under §197. The so called "bundling" rules provide that no loss deduction is allowed on the disposition of these intangible assets until all the §197 intangibles acquired in the same transaction are sold or otherwise disposed of.

Case Study 3-1

Case Study 3-1 – Dodger Manufacturing (cont.) – Intangible Assets

Assume

Returning to the example in Chapter 2, "Taxable Asset Transactions," assume that in the course of your consultations with Marichal, he mentions that he has heard about the identification of intangibles as a means of obtaining additional tax benefit in an asset purchase.

Case Study 3-1— Questions & Answers

Question 1. Based on the nature of Dodger Manufacturing Corp., discuss what types of intangible assets might be present.

Answer 1. Besides goodwill and going concern value, the types of intangible assets that might be present in Dodger Manufacturing Corp. could include the following:

- Patents
- Patent applications

Purchases Involving Intangible Assets

- Favorable leases
- Favorable contracts
- Customer lists
- Dealer networks.

Question 2. Marichal also mentions that he may be interested in including a clause in the purchase agreement whereby Koufax, Drysdale, and Podres agree not to compete with him for a five-year period within a specified geographic region. He asks what the tax consequences would be to him and the sellers under such an arrangement.

What would your response be?

Answer 2. Assuming that the covenant is respected for tax purposes, the consequences would be as follows:

- Under prior law Marichal, as the purchaser, would have amortized and received an ordinary tax deduction for the amount allocable to the covenant over its five-year term. Now he would amortize the amount allocable to the covenant over 15 years.

- The sellers (Koufax, Drysdale, and Podres) would recognize as income the amount paid for the covenant in accordance with their normal method of accounting.

Question 3. In the Chapter 2 example assume that $60,000 of the amount allocated to goodwill could be allocated to a five-year covenant not to compete. What would be the consequences to Marichal?

Answer 3. Marichal would obtain annual amortization deductions of $4,000 ($60,000 over a 15-year period). The sellers would recognize the covenant payments as ordinary income in accordance with their method of accounting.

Note that without the covenant the entire $65,000 otherwise allocable to goodwill in the Chapter 2 example would also be amortized over a 15-year period. Note also that from the sellers' standpoint gain associated with the goodwill would be capital gain, not ordinary income.

Question 4. The previous questions address intangibles from the viewpoint of the purchaser. Are there seller concerns with respect to the identification of intangible assets?

Answer 4. Yes. First, a seller can maximize the value of his/her company in the eyes of a prospective buyer by considering what intangible assets will be transferred in an asset sale. Besides goodwill and going concern value, these intangibles can include those discussed in this chapter (e.g., patents, favorable leases, customer lists, and a trained work force). Tax considerations aside, these assets may have significant value to a buyer.

From a tax perspective the identification of such assets can affect the nature of the gain or loss the seller recognizes. This remains true even after RRA of 1993. Sales proceeds attributable to goodwill and going concern value can result in a capital gain/loss.

However, this may not be true for other intangible assets. For example, software that has been amortized under the provisions of Rev. Proc. 69-21 would constitute a §1231 asset and not a capital asset. Also, transferred contracts may constitute ordinary income assets or §1231 assets. The mix of the identified assets and the portion of the sales price allocated to each under §1060 (discussed previously) should be carefully reviewed.

Chapter 4

Taxable Stock Transactions

Objective

This chapter will explain the tax considerations involved in making a taxable stock acquisition.

Introduction

In a stock disposition a shareholder has two options:

- Sell the stock in a taxable transaction, with gain or loss recognition, or

- Dispose of the stock by exchanging it for the stock of another corporation in a tax-free reorganization (reorganizations are not covered in this book).

The tax consequences of these two alternatives can be dramatically different. Generally, in a *taxable stock transaction*, the selling shareholder recognizes a gain or loss for the difference in the stock's sales price and his stock basis (§1001), and the purchaser receives a stock basis equal to what he paid for the stock. However, the tax basis of the underlying corporate assets remains undisturbed (carryover basis). This is true unless a §338 election (discussed later in this chapter) is made.

In a *tax-free reorganization* the selling shareholder recognizes no gain or loss, and he takes a basis in the acquiring company shares he receives equal to the basis he had in his old corporate shares. Similar to a taxable stock transaction, the historic tax basis of the underlying corporate assets remains undisturbed.

An important consideration in a taxable stock purchase versus a tax-free reorganization is the potential carryover of the target's "tax attributes." Tax attributes are discussed in Chapter 5, "Carryover of Tax Attributes."

Taxable Stock Sale vs. Taxable Asset Sale

A fundamental difference between a stock and an asset sale is the *corporate level tax consequences*.

- *In a stock sale*: There is no taxable income recognition to the corporation. However,

- *In an asset disposition*: The corporation recognizes gain or loss if the value of the assets differs from their tax basis.

As discussed in Chapter 2, "Taxable Asset Transactions," this is true *regardless* of whether the corporation sells its assets or distributes the assets to its shareholders.

Tax is imposed only at the *shareholder level* for stock sales. Therefore, from a tax perspective, sellers generally prefer a stock sale. If the corporation sells or distributes its assets, a second level of tax results, thus reducing the net wealth transferred to the shareholders.

Another important distinction between taxable asset sales and stock sales is that in an asset sale (purchase), target's tax attributes remain with the company and are not subject to control by the buyer. For example, as shown in Chapter 3, "Purchases Involving Intangible Assets," the selling corporation can use its net operating loss (NOL) to reduce any gain recognized on the sale of its assets. Also, a loss on the assets sold increases the selling corporation's net operating loss.

However, when a purchaser acquires target's stock, the buyer is deemed to acquire the corporate *entity* itself, not merely its assets. The tax attributes remain with the entity and effectively come under the purchaser's control.

Thus, subject to certain important restrictions (discussed in Chapter 6, "Taxable Acquisitions Involving Sole Proprietorships, S Corporations, Partnerships, and LLCs"), these attributes come under the buyer's control in a stock transaction.

Section 338 – Treating Stock Purchases as Asset Purchases

As mentioned previously, stock acquisitions do not normally result in a step-up of the company's underlying asset basis. Instead, the target's asset basis continues in effect (carryover basis). Therefore, depreciation/amortization deductions may not reflect any appreciation inherent in the purchase price.

Taxable Stock Transactions

However, §338 provides for the *elective treatment* of certain stock purchases as asset acquisitions. Section 338 uses a "deemed" or hypothetical asset sale that for tax purposes is considered to have occurred.

If the acquiring corporation makes a §338 election, then the target corporation is treated as follows:

1. As having sold all of its assets at the acquisition date for their fair market value; and

2. As a new corporation that purchased all of the assets referred to in 1. above.

Requirements for Section 338 Treatment

For the purchase of target stock to qualify for §338 treatment, the acquiring corporation must have purchased, in a taxable transaction(s) during a period of not more than twelve months, at least 80% of the voting stock and at least 80% of the total shares of all other classes of stock (except nonvoting preferred stock). If a §338 election is made, the stock sale is treated as if *Old* target sold its assets to *New* target.

Old Target's Assets Sale to New Target

Old target recognizes income to the extent that the deemed sales price exceeds *Old* target's basis in its assets. The purchaser is responsible for the payment of this tax. *New* target, as the *purchasing* corporation, is treated as a corporation with no tax attributes (earnings and profits, carryovers, etc.).

The basis allocated by New target to its assets (the *Adjusted Grossed-up Basis or AGUB*) and the sale proceeds allocated by Old target to its assets in computing gain or loss on the hypothetical asset sale (the *Modified Aggregate Deemed Sales Price or MADSP*) are based on the price paid for the target stock, plus target's liabilities at the acquisition date.

The allocation process in determining the gain recognized from the §338 election, determining the MADSP, and the new basis in the assets resulting from the election (AGUB) is the same as it is in an outright §1060 asset purchase (discussed in Chapter 2). In fact, §338 was enacted prior to §1060, and the §338 regulations are actually referred to in the §1060 language.

Primary Drawbacks of the Section 338 Election

The two primary drawbacks of the §338 election are as follows:

- *Old* target tax recognizes income to the extent that the deemed sales price exceeds *Old* target's basis in its assets, and

- Any target tax attributes not used in target's final tax return are lost.

Note that the *purchaser* cannot use its NOL to offset any gain recognized in the transaction.

While §338 elections were popular in the early 1980s, their usefulness has been severely limited.

Under the repeal of the so-called General Utilities doctrine, the taxable income triggered from the §338 election is equal to the basis step-up (e.g., the full extent to which fair market value exceeds basis). From a time-value-of-money standpoint it makes little sense to trigger immediate taxable gain to increase taxable basis by the same amount, and, therefore, generate additional deductions over an extended period of time (via amortization and depreciation).

Tax Planning: Target with Unused NOL

An exception to the above discussion involves a target that has an unused NOL. As mentioned above, target's tax attributes disappear after a §338 election is made.

However, under §382 (dealing with NOL carryovers, as discussed more fully in Chapter 6), target is allowed to offset gain on a §338 election with its NOL in its final return (any unused remaining NOL carryforward is lost subsequent to the election).

Therefore, in situations where target has an NOL approximately equal to the gain that would be triggered from the election, a §338 election should be considered, since an effectively tax-free step-up can be achieved. Note that the purchaser cannot use its own NOL to offset the gain recognized when a section 338 election is made.

The Section 338(h)(10) Alternative

Another possible use of §338 involves the special §338(h)(10) election. Section 338(h)(10) allows the acquiring company and target's parent company, under certain conditions, to electively treat the sale of target's stock as an asset sale that occurs while target is part of the selling corporation's tax group.

Like the "regular" §338 election discussed previously, the §338(h)(10) election involves an election to treat a stock sale as if an asset sale has occurred. However, the consequences of a §338(h)(10) election can be dramatically different from a "regular" §338 election.

New Selling Corporation's Responsibilities on a Target's Stock Sale

Under §338(h)(10) the sale of target's stock is treated as though target's assets have been sold to the acquiring corporation. Thus, the *selling corporation* (and not the acquiring corporation) is responsible for the tax liability on the hypothetical asset sale. (Compare this to a regular §338 election where the purchaser is responsible for target's tax on the deemed asset sale). Section 338(h)(10) also provides that any gain that would have been recognized by the selling corporation on the actual stock sale is ignored.

Taxable Stock Transactions

Acquirer's Basis in Target's Assets

The acquiring corporation's basis in target's assets is adjusted under Regs. §1.338(h)(10) 1T(e)(6). These rules provide that like the regular §338 election, the AGUB (based primarily on the price paid for target's stock) must be determined.

As with the regular §338 election, target recognizes gain or loss on the hypothetical asset disposition to the extent that the modified aggregate deemed sales price (*MADSP* discussed previously) exceeds its tax basis in its assets. If target and the selling corporation file a consolidated tax return, this gain (or loss) is recognized while target is a member of the tax group.

A §338(h)(10) election allows the purchaser a stepped-up asset basis while making the seller responsible for the tax on the deemed asset sale. Because of the unique nature of the election (which must be made jointly by the buyer and seller), it can reduce the seller's after-tax cost of the sale. This reduction in tax liability may be passed on to the purchaser through a negotiated reduction in the stock's sales price. Since the seller and acquirer must jointly agree to make the §338(h)(10) election, a review of the tax consequences suggests when it is preferable to make the election.

Acquirer's Basis in Target's Stock

The acquirer's basis in target's stock is its cost. If no §338(h)(10) election (or a regular §338 election) is made, and target's stock is held indefinitely, this cost basis will not yield a tax benefit to the acquirer. Target's historical tax basis in its assets carries over and target continues to depreciate and amortize its assets on this basis. Target's tax attributes are available for carryover, subsequent to the purchase, subject to the restrictions of §§381, 382, 384, 269, and the consolidated tax return rules (discussed in Chapter 6).

Tax Consequences to Acquirer and Seller

The §338(h)(10), election creates significantly different tax consequences to the acquirer and the seller. The acquirer's basis in the assets is stepped up under the AGUB rules. Target recognizes gain or loss to the extent that the allocated MADSP is greater (or less) than its basis in the assets. If target and the seller (its parent corporation) are filing a consolidated tax return, this gain (or loss) is recognized while target is a member of the seller's tax group.

As with the regular §338 election, target can use its NOLs (if any) to offset any gain recognized in connection with the deemed asset sale. However, *unlike the regular §338 election, target's unused tax attributes do not disappear*; target is deemed to be liquidated into its parent (the seller) who inherits its tax attributes.

When to Use the Election

Under §338(h)(10), gain on the deemed asset sale may or may not differ significantly from the amount of gain that would be recognized by the seller without the election. Absent the election, the seller (target's parent) recognizes gain to the extent that the price paid for target's stock exceeds its basis in target's stock. If the potential gain at target's level on the deemed asset sale differs significantly from the potential gain at the seller's level on the actual stock sale, the §338(h)(10) election may be more or less desirable.

Similarly, the extent of target's and the seller's NOLs (if any) will influence the election decision. Target could use its restricted NOLs to offset any gain on the deemed asset sale. To the contrary, if the seller has substantial restricted NOLs, it may favor a stock sale without the §338(h)(10) election.

Thus, there are a number of considerations in deciding when to utilize the §338(h)(10) election. These include the following:

- The extent of target's and the seller's NOLs;

- The difference between the deemed sales price (MADSP) of target's assets and its basis in those assets; and

- The difference between the sales price of target's stock and the basis the seller has in that stock.

Another consideration in making the election is the nature of target's other tax attributes. These tax attributes pass to the seller under the §338(h)(l0) election alternative. State and local tax consequences should also be considered.

The removal of the capital gains preferential tax rate treatment for corporations will make the §338(h)(l0) election and direct asset acquisitions more appealing to the corporate sellers, since the gain on asset and stock dispositions is taxed at the same rate. The §338(h)(l0) election alternative can be more easily accomplished than a direct asset purchase, since it involves a stock sale that is only *electively* treated as an asset acquisition.

The potential advantages of the §338(h)(10) election should be carefully explored by both the acquirer and the seller. If the aggregate tax position of the parties can be enhanced through the election, this benefit can be a significant negotiating point in an acquisition.

Allocation and Reporting Requirements

As discussed in Chapter 2, special allocation and information reporting rules apply to *asset acquisitions* that are subject to §1060. The information reporting rules of §1060 do not apply to an acquisition of a trade or business that is structured as a *stock acquisition* if the transferee does not elect under §338 to treat the stock purchase as an asset acquisition.

In the case of a stock purchase where a §338(h)(10) election is made, the purchasing corporation and the selling consolidated group must report information with respect to the consideration received in the transaction at such time and in such manner as provided in regulations under §338. In general, the reporting and allocation rules of §1060 do not apply in any case in which a stock purchase is treated as an asset purchase under §338.

Where a person holds at least a 10% interest in the value of an entity and both transfers an interest in the entity and enters into an employment contract, covenant not to compete, royalty, lease agreement, or other agreement with the transferee, such person and the transferee must report the information concerning the transaction at such time and in such manner as the IRS may require by regulations.

Section 338 Regulations

The prior §338 regulations were criticized for the complexity created by the "consistency" provisions. Broadly speaking, the consistency rules were enacted to prevent taxpayers from selectively acquiring assets and stock from a target with the intent of circumventing the application of §338. These regulations also contained various elections to be made in the event that a qualified stock purchase occurred but the taxpayer did not wish to have §338 apply (this was usually the case, given the repeal of the General Utilities doctrine).

The prior regulations contained a serious trap for the unwary. For example, an asset purchase from an affiliate of a company whose stock was also purchased by a buyer could trigger a "deemed" §338 election with respect to the stock purchase. This could generate disastrous tax consequences for the buyer.

Regulations proposed in 1992 and adopted in 1994 have simplified the previous approach to dealing with the consistency issue. Generally, these regulations provide that no election under §338 is deemed made or required with respect to any acquired company or affiliate of the acquired company. Instead, the company acquiring an asset in such a situation may have a carryover basis in that asset. However, those advisors involved in stock acquisitions should review these regulations to avoid any unexpected consequences of their application.

Summary

This chapter has reviewed the tax consequences of a taxable stock acquisition.

Section 338 allows a stock purchase to be electively treated as though the purchaser has acquired assets. In this event the purchaser is responsible for the tax triggered on the hypothetical asset sale. Target's tax attributes do not carry over to the purchaser. Instead, they are deemed to disappear after the transaction is completed.

"Regular" §338 elections seldom are desirable. The cost of the basis step-up is the triggering of taxable income equal to the step-up amount. From a time-value-of-money concept, it does not make sense to gain a tax basis that can yield deductions only over time (i.e., amortization and depreciation) at the cost of paying an immediate tax equal to these future tax savings.

An alternative to the "regular" §338 election is the §338(h)(10) election. Under this special election (which differs in numerous ways from the regular §338 election), the target's parent corporation is responsible for the tax on the deemed asset sale. The target's tax attributes carry over to the selling parent. The seller recognizes a gain on the deemed asset sale, and its actual gain on the stock sale is ignored.

The specific circumstances of a transaction should be reviewed to determine if either §338 election is desirable.

Stock acquisitions also permit the acquirer (subject to certain limitations) access to target's tax attributes (e.g., NOL carryovers). This aspect of stock acquisitions is discussed in Chapter 6.

Case Study 4-1

Case Study 4-1 — Dodger Manufacturing (cont.)

Review the facts of the Dodger Manufacturing Case Study before proceeding.

Case Study 4-1 — Questions & Answers

Question 1. Consider again the Dodger Manufacturing example discussed in Chapter 2. Let us assume that a sale of stock is the agreed upon method:

   a. What would be the tax effect to the stockholders if they sell their stock for $360,000 payable in cash and/or other property? (Assume the alternative minimum tax is not a factor and the applicable capital gains rate is 20%.)

   b. If the stockholders of Dodger Manufacturing Corporation receive none or only part of the selling price of their stock in the year of sale, can they pay tax on the installment method?

Answer 1. a. If the stockholders sell their stock for cash and/or other property, they realize a taxable capital gain.

Taxable Stock Transactions

The tax on this transaction would be computed as follows:

Selling price	$360,000
Basis of stock	100,000
Gain	$260,000
Tax ($260,000 × 20%) =	$ 52,000
Net proceeds (360,000 less 52,000)	$308,000

The stockholders' net proceeds are greater in the stock sale than in the asset sale discussed in Chapter 2. This is the main reason why sellers normally prefer a stock sale to an asset sale.

Note: The actual tax paid by each stockholder will obviously depend on several variables:

- What other capital gains and losses each stockholder has in the same year to offset or augment the above gains;

- The effect of installment reporting; and/or

- The stockholder's individual tax situation.

b. Yes. Referring to the previous discussion (see Chapter 2 for a discussion of the installment sale rules), the sale of stock by the shareholders should qualify for installment sale treatment (the stock in this example is not publicly traded).

While the installment method can defer shareholder gain recognition, it also results in the shareholder not receiving all the cash for his stock immediately.

Note that each stockholder's decision to accept either all or defer part of his sales price to another year is not affected by the decisions or actions of the other stockholders. While the purchaser may pay 100% of the total selling price to one stockholder, any other stockholder receiving less than 100% of his selling price in the year of sale may still use the installment method.

For example, Podres, who owns 20% of the outstanding stock, wishes payment in full (20% of $360,000 = $72,000) and Koufax and Drysdale accept 40% of the selling price in the year of sale [40% of (80% × $360,000) = $115,200], the payment in the year of sale to all stockholders would be $187,200 or 52% of the total selling price. Koufax and

Drysdale would be required to report their gains on the installment method (unless they elect out of the method).

	% Owned	Amount Entitled to	% Received	Received in Year of Sale	Installment Method Applicable
Podres	20%	$ 72,000	100%	$ 72,000	No
Koufax	50%	180,000	40%	72,000	Yes*
Drysdale	30%	108,000	40%	43,200	Yes*
TOTALS	100%	$360,000		$187,200	

Question 2. Willie Marichal is considering having his corporation (P) purchase the Dodger stock and make a §338 election, which allows the stock purchase to electively be treated as an asset purchase.

What would the tax consequences be?

Does the election make "tax sense" in this case?

Answer 2. This election provides a method for obtaining a stepped-up asset basis from a stock purchase provided that certain conditions of the tax law are met. However, unlike a simple stock purchase, target's tax attributes disappear after the election is made.

A §338 election would result in a stepped-up basis for the assets of Dodger if the acquiring corporation, P, followed these specific steps:

- P must purchase at least 80% of target's stock (voting and all other classes except nonvoting preferred) within a twelve-month period; and

- Not later than the 15th day of the ninth month following the qualifying stock purchase, an election must be made for the stock purchase to be treated under §338.

The assets would have a stepped-up basis determined by allocating the purchase price of the stock (plus adjustment for liabilities) among the various assets of Dodger according to their fair market values. This procedure follows the values discussed for asset purchases in Chapter 2. As long as the acquiring corporation, P, makes an election by the fifteenth day of the ninth month after the month of such acquisition, it could allocate the purchase price of the stock to the various assets held by Dodger.

The basis allocated by New target to its assets is based on the price paid for target stock, plus liabilities of target at the acquisition date.

Taxable Stock Transactions

Marichal's Corporation P, as the purchaser, would be liable for tax on the difference between the fair market value of the assets and their tax basis. In this example, the "regular" §338 election does not make tax sense, since Dodger has no NOL to offset the taxable gain generated.

Note that for Marichal to consider making the regular §338 election or a §338(h)(10) election (discussed below) he would have to have his controlled corporation make the purchase (only corporate, not individual, purchasers qualify for §338 elections).

Question 3. Marichal wants to purchase the stock of Dodger Manufacturing Corporation and make a §338(h)(10) election. (Assume for this question that Dodger is the subsidiary of a corporate parent with which Marichal is negotiating.)

What factors should be considered?

Answer 3. If the parent of Dodger has a low basis in its Dodger stock (while Dodger has a high basis in its assets), the election might make sense. This is because the §338(h)(10) election allows the corporate seller to ignore the actual gain on the stock sale at the expense of recognizing the gain on the hypothetical sale of Dodger's assets to the acquiring corporation (note that here, as in the regular §338 election, a corporate acquirer is required).

The election might also make sense if Dodger has an existing NOL, which could be used to offset any gain deemed to be realized on the hypothetical asset sale.

From Marichal's standpoint, if a §338(h)(10) election can reduce the gain Dodger's parent will recognize on the sale, this could lead to a negotiated lower price for the Dodger stock. However, it should at least encourage the seller to join in making the election, which will give Marichal's Corporation a stepped up tax basis in the assets. Note that both the acquirer and seller must join in making the election.

Question 4. What other tax consideration should be considered by Marichal in acquiring the stock of the corporation?

Answer 4. One consideration is the tax attributes of the target corporation. Such attributes (e.g., earnings and profits, NOLs, credits, etc.) are not a concern in asset purchases, since attributes do not follow the assets in an asset sale. Subject to certain limitations, however, the tax attributes do in effect flow to the purchaser, since the purchaser acquires the target corporation. More is said of this in Chapter 6.

Chapter 5

Carryover of Tax Attributes

Introduction

The purpose of this chapter is to review those provisions that impact the carryover of target's tax attributes. A target's tax attributes never carry over in a *taxable asset* acquisition. However, they can carry over in a *taxable stock* acquisition, subject to various restrictions. This chapter discusses tax attribute carryovers relating to taxable stock acquisitions.

The net-operating loss (NOL) is typically the most sought-after target tax attribute, since it can potentially *offset* otherwise taxable income. In the past taxpayers frequently entered into transactions, not for business reasons, but to acquire a target's NOL. To curb this so called "trafficking" in NOLs, Congress enacted several provisions.

The ability to use a target corporation's NOL is an important consideration in a stock acquisition. For this reason, we will spend some time discussing the relevant rules.

Section 382

Section 382 provides special limitations on NOL carryovers when there has been more than a 50% "ownership change" of a "loss corporation," resulting (broadly speaking) from either a taxable stock purchase or a tax-free transaction.

Note that there are many terms specifically defined for purposes of §382. The §382 rules are quite complex and this chapter will not be a complete discussion of these rules. However, this chapter will explain the basic rules and the issues relevant to the purchase of a business. Also keep in mind the overall purpose of §382 is to provide an objective test to see if there has been a significant change in ownership of a corporation with a tax NOL, and to impose limitations on the use of the NOL by those increasing their ownership in the corporation.

We'll first discuss the definitions of an "owner shift" and "equity structure shift" and the relevant testing periods, and then discuss how a 5% shareholder is defined for purposes of §382.

A **loss corporation** is defined under §382(k)(1) as a corporation entitled to use a net operating loss carryover or having a net operating loss for the tax year in which the ownership change occurs. A net operating loss is essentially a tax loss of the corporate entity that is available for carry back or carry over to other tax years of the corporate entity.

A loss corporation can also include a corporation with a "net unrealized built-in loss" (see later discussion in this chapter).

An "ownership change" can result from either an "owner shift involving a 5% shareholder" or an "equity structure shift."

Owner Shifts

"Owner shifts" can result from purchases, sales, redemptions, and §351 (incorporation) transactions. However, they will not occur because of the following:

- Fluctuations in value;

- Transfers between non-5% shareholders; and

- Transfers that occur by reason of death, gift, divorce, or bequest.

Under §382(g)(2) owner shifts involving 5% shareholders include a taxable purchase of the NOL company's stock by a person who is a 5% shareholder before the purchase, or a taxable stock purchase by a person who becomes a 5% shareholder by reason of the purchase.

Equity Structure Shifts

Note. An ownership change can also result from an "equity structure shift."

Equity structure shifts are defined in §382(g)(3) as all tax-free reorganizations defined in subparagraphs A, B, C, and E of §368(a)(1) and some tax-free reorganizations defined in subparagraphs D and G of §368(a)(1). Under §382(g)(3), equity structure shifts also include public stock offerings not involving 5% shareholders.

Since this book does not cover acquisitions of a business through reorganizations, just keep in mind that §382 can also operate to limit the utilization of the NOL of a company acquired through a reorganization.

Testing Periods

Whether an ownership change has occurred is evaluated over a *testing period*; it is not based solely on a single transaction. The testing period is generally defined as the three-year period that ends on the date of any owner shift involving a 5% shareholder.

However, this testing period can be less than three years when an ownership change has already occurred, and the testing period used in determining whether a subsequent ownership change has occurred does not begin prior to the first day following the previous ownership change.

Example 5-1

Assume an ownership change occurs on July 15, 2004.

An owner shift involving a 5% shareholder occurs on February 5, 2005.

The appropriate testing period for measuring whether an ownership change occurred on February 5, 2005, begins on July 16, 2004, and ends on February 5, 2005.

Also, the testing period cannot begin on the earlier of the

- First day of the first tax year from which a loss is being carried; or

- First day of the tax year in which the testing event occurs.

Example 5-2

Assume a corporation was profitable until 2004 when it incurred an NOL.

The NOL carries forward to 2005.

Further assume that an owner shift involving a 5% shareholder occurs on February 1, 2005.

In this case the testing date begins on January 1, 2004.

Losses Limited by Section 382

Generally the §382 rules limit the utilization of two types of losses.

- Most importantly, §382 limits NOL carryforwards that arise prior to the ownership change.

- Section 382 also limits the utilization of **built-in losses**. Section 382(h) defines built-in losses as the excess of the tax basis of the corporation's assets over their aggregate fair market value measured on the date of the ownership change (however, a *de minimis* rule applies in determining whether or not a built-in loss exists). Keep in mind also that the built-in loss limitations rules do not apply unless, at the time the ownership change occurs, the total fair market value of all the corporation's assets is less than the total tax basis of its assets.

Example 5-3

Assume M corporation has a calendar year-end.

On June 30 it undergoes an ownership change.

Its current year NOL is $700,000 and its NOL carryover from prior years is $2,000,000.

Question

What is the NOL subject to limitation under §382?

Discussion

In this example the NOL subject to limitation is $2,349,041.

It is equal to the $2,000,000 carryforward, plus a pro rata share (700,000 × 182/365 days) of the current year loss.

NOLs subject to the §382 limitation include NOLs incurred in the year of change, but allocable to the period on or before the ownership change date.

Note. In this example a pro-ration of the loss in the year of ownership change was used. However, §382 also provides for an elective closing of the books to measure the NOL incurred prior to the ownership change.

Carryover of Tax Attributes

Example 5-4

Assume Alpha Corporation has the following balance sheet immediately prior to an ownership change:

Assets and Liabilities

	Basis	Fair Market Value
Cash	$ 200	$ 200
Accounts Receivable	2,000	1,700
Inventory	3,000	2,000
Equipment	2,000	1,000
Total assets	7,200	$4,900
Liabilities	(3,000)	(3,000)
Net Worth	$4,200	$1,900

Discussion

In this example the built-in loss is $2,300.

This is computed as $7,200 of asset basis, less the assets' fair market value of $4,900.

Five-Percent Shareholders

Section 382 specifically addresses any "5% shareholder" whose interest in the NOL company has increased by more than 50% within the testing period. Generally, all shareholders that own less than 5% of the NOL company's stock are deemed to be collectively a single 5% shareholder.

A 5% shareholder is defined to be one of the following:

- An individual owns (directly or indirectly) 5% or more of a loss corporation at any time during the testing period; or

- A public group.

Special rules concerning 5% shareholders:

- A "public group" refers to individuals or other tax entities each of whom owns 5% of a loss corporation. Special rules provide for either aggregating or segregating public

5-5

groups and for determining whether or not an owner shift or an equity structure shift has occurred.

- In determining whether an individual has indirect stock ownership, the §318 attribution rules are utilized. The §382 regulations also provide entity to individual attribution, including special option attribution rules.

- In determining whether an ownership change has occurred, the ownership increases of all 5% shareholders are considered in the aggregate.

- Under §382(k)(6) the 5% shareholder test and the 50% ownership change test are computed based on ownership values, not on voting interests.

The following examples illustrate the §382 rules:

Example 5-5

On January 1, 2004, the stock of L corporation is publicly traded; no shareholder holds five percent or more of L stock.

On September 1, 2004, individuals A, B, and C, who were not previously L shareholders and are unrelated to each other or to any L shareholders, each acquire one-third of L.

Discussion

A, B, and C each have become 5% shareholders of L and, in the aggregate, hold 100 percent of the L stock.

Accordingly, an *ownership change has occurred*, because the *percentage of L stock* owned by the three 5% shareholders after the ownership (100%) *has increased* by more than 50 percentage points over the lowest percentage of L stock owned by A, B, and C at any time during the testing period (0% prior to September 1, 2004).

> **Example 5-6**
>
> On January 1, 2003, L corporation is wholly owned by individual X.
>
> On January 1, 2004, X sells 50% of his stock to 1,000 shareholders, all of whom are unrelated to him.
>
> On January 1, 2005, X sells his remaining 50% interest to an additional 1,000 shareholders, all of whom are also unrelated to him.
>
> **Discussion**
>
> Based on these facts, *there is no ownership change immediately following the initial sales by X*, because the *percentage of L stock* owned by the group of less than 5% shareholders (who are treated as a single 5% shareholder) after the ownership (50%) *has not increased* by more than 50 percentage points over the lowest percentage of stock owned by this group at any time during the testing period (0% prior to January 1, 2004).
>
> On January 1, 2005, however, *there is an ownership change*, because the *percentage of stock owned* by the group of less than 5% shareholders after the ownership (100%) *has increased* by more than 50 percentage points over their lowest percentage ownership at any time during the testing period (0% prior to January 1, 2004).

Impact If Section 382 Applies

If an ownership change occurs, the amount of loss that can be used each year to offset post-acquisition income is *limited* to a published long-term tax-exempt rate, as defined in §382(f), multiplied by the *value* of the NOL company at the acquisition date.

> **Example 5-7**
>
> Assume an individual purchases 100% of the stock of target corporation.
>
> An ownership change has occurred with respect to target. Assume that at the time of the acquisition, target has a value of $15,000,000 and has a pre-acquisition NOL of $140,000,000.
>
> Assume further that the applicable federal tax rate is 8%.
>
> **Result**
>
> In this case the maximum amount of target's NOL that can be used each year under the §382 rules is $1,200,000 (8% x $15,000,000).

However, §382(c) disallows all NOL carryovers if the acquiring company does not continue substantially the same trade or business of the NOL company for two years after the acquisition. The annual §382 limitation is effectively "zero" if the requirement is not met.

This requirement is satisfied if the corporation either:

- Continues the old loss corporation's business (regulations provide that if the old loss corporation had more than one line of business, a significant line of business must be continued); or

- Continues to use a significant portion of the loss corporation's assets in a business.

Other Rules

Section 382 also has special provisions to prohibit potential circumvention of the NOL limitations.

These provisions include the following:

- Reduction in value for capital contributions to the NOL company for purposes of increasing its value;

- Reduction in value for the NOL company having substantial nonbusiness assets immediately after the ownership change; and

- Recognition of built-in gains and losses.

Recognition of Built-in Gains and Losses

There are special rules related to the use of a "built-in loss" and a "built-in gain" of a target corporation with NOLs (i.e., a loss corporation). If a target loss corporation has a net unrealized built-in loss at the time the ownership change occurs, any loss recognized within a five-year period, beginning at the time of the acquisition, is subject to the §382 limitations.

However, if the target loss corporation has a net unrealized built-in gain, the §382 limitation otherwise applicable is increased by any gain recognized within a five-year recognition period.

Under §382 a "net unrealized built-in gain" occurs when the fair market value of target's assets immediately before the acquisition (i.e., the ownership change), exceeds the aggregate adjusted tax basis of those assets. To the contrary, a "net unrealized built-in loss" is the amount by which the total tax basis of the target's assets exceeds their value. Section 382 provides that in computing these amounts, the target's assets are not deemed to include cash, cash-like items, or marketable securities that have neither substantially appreciated nor depreciated.

It is the *recognition* of the built-in gains or built-in losses that triggers the special §382 rules.

Recognized Built-in Gain

A *recognized* built-in gain is defined as any gain recognized during the five-year post-acquisition period from the sale of an asset that was held by the target immediately before the acquisition, to the extent the gain does not exceed the excess of the value over the asset's tax basis *at the acquisition date*. However, the increase in the §382 limitation cannot be greater than the original net unrealized gain, reduced by any recognized built-in gains.

Recognized Built-in Loss

A recognized built-in loss is any loss recognized during the same five-year period on the sale of an asset held by the target at the time of the acquisition, to the extent the loss does not exceed the excess of the asset's tax basis over its value *at the acquisition date*. Such losses are treated as pre-acquisition losses and are subject to the §382 limitations.

Since the determination of a net unrealized built-in gain or loss is important, a valuation of the target's assets may be required. However, to limit the need for such valuations, §382 provides that a target's net unrealized gain or loss is deemed to be zero unless the gain (or the loss) exceeds the lesser of either of the following:

- 15% of the value of the target's assets immediately prior to the acquisition;
- $10,000,000.

Section 383

Section 383 extends the §382 limitations for NOL carryovers to carryovers of unused general business credits, foreign tax credits, minimum tax credits, and capital loss carryforwards.

Separate Return Limitation Years ("SRLYs")

Regulations §1.150221(c) provides limitations on the deductibility of NOL carryovers from separate return limitation years (SRLYs). Regulations §1.15021(f) defines a *separate return limitation year* as any separate return year of a member of a consolidated return group or the predecessor company of any such member.

Limitations on Carrybacks and Carryovers

A SRLY limits the use of certain carrybacks and carryovers, specifically,

- The net operating loss;
- The capital loss; and

- The foreign tax credit.

The SRLY limitation may also apply to other carryovers, such as research and development credits and targeted jobs credits (*Wegman's Properties Inc.*, 78 TC 786).

Limitations on Built-in Deductions

The SRLY concept is intended to prevent the misuse of preaffiliation losses. The SRLY rules also limit the utilization of certain "built-in deductions."

These are losses economically incurred in a SRLY, which are not *recognized* until the current consolidation year because they were recognized in a separate return year and carried over to the current year. Their deductibility is generally limited by the SRLY rules.

Section 269

Section 269(a) provides that if there has been an *acquisition by any person of control* of a corporation, *or an acquisition by a corporation* of the *property* of a previously uncontrolled corporation with such property taking the transferor's basis, and if the *"principal purpose"* for the *acquisition* is the evasion or avoidance of federal income taxes by securing the benefit of a deduction, credit, or other allowance that would not otherwise be enjoyed, *then* such deduction, credit, or other allowance is disallowed. Control is defined as 50% or more in value of the stock or 50% or more of the voting power of the corporation.

Since application of §269 involves a facts and circumstance determination, care should be exercised when such a situation presents itself.

Determining Whether Section 269 Applies

Knowledge of the tax consequences at the time of the acquisition is a consideration in determining whether §269 will be applied. For example, the Tax Court denied NOL carryovers where the taxpayer originally negotiated for assets and bought the stock after learning of the tax advantages (*Huddle, Inc.*, TC Memo 1961150).

Where the facts indicate that at the time of the acquisition no thought was given to the tax consequences, tax avoidance was ruled not to have been the principal purpose for the acquisition [*Hawaiian Trust Co., Ltd.*, 291 F. 2d 761 (9th Cir. 1961)].

More recent cases suggest that as taxpayers have become more sophisticated, the courts expect them to be knowledgeable of the tax consequences. Therefore, such knowledge per se is no longer a conclusive factor.

Taxpayers have prevailed in showing a principal business purpose for an acquisition in the following situations, among others:

- Acquisition of like manufacturing company because of insufficient manufacturing facilities (Superior Garment Co., TC Memo 1965283).

- Expansion into states where markets have been developed by target company [*Clarksdale Rubber Co.*, 45 TC 234 (1965)].

Section 269(b)

Section 269(b) addresses *subsidiary liquidations*. For §269(b) to apply, the following conditions must be satisfied:

- There must be a qualified stock purchase as defined under §338 (broadly speaking, this requires a taxable acquisition of 80% or more of the target stock within a twelve-month period);

- An election is not be made under §338 with respect to the stock purchase;

- Target is liquidated into its new parent subsequent to a plan of liquidation adopted within two years after the acquisition date; and

- The principal purpose for the liquidation is the evasion or avoidance of federal income taxes.

It is important to note for §269(b) purposes that, unlike the §269(a) provisions, the principal purpose of the liquidation and not of the original acquisition is of critical importance.

Section 269 has usually been applied in cases where a profitable company acquires a loss company in an attempt to avail itself of its NOL.

Note. Section 382 now provides a mechanical objective test to supplement the "facts and circumstances" approval of §269 in curbing such transactions.

Section 269 has also been applied to situations where a *loss* company a*cquires a profitable company*. However, Congress was concerned with the IRS's lack of judicial success in attacking this type of acquisition and legislated §384.

Section 384

Section 384 deals with these situations in which target companies with built-in gains are acquired by loss companies seeking to offset their losses against the acquired company's built-in gains.

Section 384 provides limits on the use of pre-acquisition losses to avoid tax on the target's built-in gains. The rules apply to both stock and asset acquisitions.

Stock Acquisitions

With respect to *stock acquisitions*, §384 applies if a corporation acquires control of a target (either directly or indirectly) and either corporation has built-in gains. The control requirements are met if a corporation owns stock representing 80% or more of the total voting power and 80% or more of the total value of the stock of another corporation.

Section 384 employs a five-year post-acquisition recognition period and a realized built-in gain/loss concept similar to that used in §382. Generally, income that relates to the recognition of built-in gains can only be offset by the pre-acquisition losses of the gain corporation. A **gain corporation** is defined as any corporation with net unrealized built-in gains.

Asset Acquisitions

Generally, if a corporation has a net unrealized built-in gain, gain on any asset recognized during the five-year post-acquisition period will be presumed to be subject to the rules, and thus, such gain may not offset any pre-acquisition NOLs. However, under §384(c) taxpayers can overcome this presumption by demonstrating that the asset giving rise to the gain was not held by the corporation at the time of the acquisition or, for assets held at the time of the acquisition, that the gain is attributable to post-acquisition appreciation. Section 384(c) also provides that pre-acquisition losses include net unrealized built-in losses of the NOL corporation that are recognized during the five-year post-acquisition period.

Other Considerations

Section 384(c) also provides that the term "recognized built-in gains" is deemed to include any item of income attributable to periods prior to the acquisition. Such pre-acquisition income items must also be considered in determining if the corporation has any net unrealized built-in gains.

Similar to the built-in gain rules discussed earlier in connection with §382, the §384 recognized built-in gain for any year cannot be more than the total net unrealized built-in gain, less all recognized built-in gains accounted for in prior recognition periods.

Section 384(b) provides an exception to the application of §384. Section 384 will not apply when the gain corporation and the corporation with the pre-acquisition loss are members of the same "controlled group" for five years prior to the acquisition. Common control is defined as 50% or more of stock ownership.

The IRS has authority to promulgate regulations to prevent taxpayers from avoiding application of the §384 rules [§384(f)]. Also, as mentioned above, §384 applies to the built-in gains of either the acquiring company or the target company. This restricts a corporation's ability to offset built-in gains with pre-acquisition losses of an acquired company.

Summary

This chapter contains a discussion of the tax law restrictions placed on a purchaser's ability to acquire the NOLs and other tax attributes of a target company. The provisions discussed include §§269, 382, 383, 384, and the consolidated tax return rules. All of these rules should be considered when either a stock purchase or tax-free reorganization is contemplated.

- Specifically, §269 disallows tax benefits to an acquirer in a transaction that is primarily tax-motivated. Section 269 requires a determination of the purchaser's intent, and therefore, depends on the facts and circumstances of a particular situation.

- Unlike §269 (which is subjective in nature) §382 involves mechanical rules for determining the extent to which NOLs of a target company are available to the purchaser. Section 382 applies to both stock purchases and certain tax-free reorganizations. These rules limit the utilization of an NOL to an amount based on the value of the acquired company at the time of the acquisition. Section 383 extends these limitations to certain tax credits.

- Section 384 limits the ability of a loss company to offset its NOLs against the built-in gains recognized (post-acquisition) by a target company.

- The SRLY provisions limit utilization of the target company's pre-acquisition losses, which may be offset against the income of an acquirer. Essentially, these rules limit the utilization of an acquired company's NOLs to the extent of its post-acquisition income. The above restrictions must be considered in determining which tax attributes of a target company can provide a post-acquisition benefit to an acquirer. Note that one or more of the restrictions can apply to a particular transaction, and the available tax attributes (e.g., NOLs) can be severely limited or eliminated.

Case Study 5-1

Case Study 5-1 — Mad Max Electronics Company

Assume

You are the CPA and tax consultant for Mad Max Electronics Co. (Mad Max), which imports, distributes, and sells foreign compact disc players and parts. Mad Max was formed in 1996 and has shown consistent profits in each year of operation.

Max Manilow, president of Mad Max, stops at your office to discuss the possible acquisition of a corporation with a large tax NOL.

The company for sale, Edsel Record Players, Inc. (Edsel), operates in the same city as Mad Max; it has an NOL carryover of $200,000 as of December 31, 2005, from post2000 tax years. Edsel distributes domestic turntables and maintains a service and repair department for all makes of turntables. It enjoys a fine reputation, earned through providing excellent service to its customers. It has only one class of stock outstanding.

Manilow is anxious to acquire Edsel's service and repair departments. He believes that the reputation of Edsel's service and its customer list will be valuable to Mad Max, and that the service department could be restructured to provide repair service on CD players as well as turntables.

He asks for your advice in acquiring Edsel Record Players so that he can obtain the benefit of the NOL.

(Assume the date of acquisition will be September 30, 2006, that Edsel's loss from January 1 to September 30, 2006, is $150,000 and that both Mad Max and Edsel are calendar-year taxpayers.)

Case Study 5-1 — Questions & Answers

Question 1. In general, what are the tax considerations that could be relevant to the post-acquisition survival of Edsel's pre-acquisition NOL?

Answer 1. The tax law presents a number of restrictions on the utilization of an acquired company's NOL carryovers. These include the following:

- Section 269(a) dealing with tax-motivated acquisitions [and §269(b) dealing with tax-motivated subsidiary liquidations];

- Section 382, dealing with limitations on the use of NOLs of acquired corporations, based on the value of the company at acquisition; and

Carryover of Tax Attributes

- The consolidated tax return SRLY rules that, in general, indicate that NOLs of acquired companies can only be offset against income generated by these companies.

- Section 384, dealing with limitations on using NOLs to offset built-in gains.

One or more of these provisions may be applicable to a given transaction. Consequently, all of these provisions should be considered in determining the extent to which the pre-acquisition NOLs of a target are available to an acquirer.

The applicability of these provisions to the Edsel acquisition is discussed in greater detail in the following questions.

Question 2. Mad Max might prefer to purchase the assets of Edsel. Can it retain the NOL carryover if it purchases assets?

Answer 2. No. The carryovers are tax attributes unique to Edsel as a corporate entity. For Mad Max to acquire these attributes, it must either purchase Edsel stock or it must acquire Edsel through a nontaxable reorganization to which §381(a) applies. The tax attributes will remain with Edsel if it simply sells its assets.

Question 3. If Mad Max purchases all of Edsel's stock:

- What is the annual NOL limitation as computed under §382, assuming Edsel is valued at $400,000 and the long-term tax-exempt rate is 5%?

- What is the total amount of Edsel's NOL?

- Would a §338 or §338(h)(10) election benefit Mad Max?

Answer 3. Annual NOL Limitation. *Since the acquisition of Edsel constitutes an ownership involving a 5% shareholder, the §382 rules would be triggered. The annual limitation would be as follows:*

Valuation of Edsel at the date of the owner shift	$400,000
Assumed long-term tax-exempt rate	× 5%
Amount of Edsel's NOL that could be utilized per year against Mad Max's taxable income	$ 20,000

Edsel would also have to meet the requirements of §382(c) regarding the two-year post-acquisition continuity of business enterprise. If the continuity of business enterprise test is not satisfied, all of the NOL carryover would be disallowed. However, this does not appear to be a problem in this case.

Total NOL

Amount of yearly NOL utilized (from above)	$ 20,000
Maximum NOL carryover period in years	× 15
Total amount of Edsel's NOL to be utilized	$300,000
Edsel's NOL carrying into 1995	$200,000
Edsel's losses from 1/1/96 9/30/96	150,000
Total amount of Edsel's NOL	$350,000

Tax Planning: Section 338 or §338(h)(10) Election. Based on the above calculations, §382 would not allow Mad Max to receive benefit for at least $50,000 of Edsel's NOL. Mad Max may want to consider a §338 election or a §338(h)(10) election to potentially utilize the full amount of the NOL (see discussion in Chapter 5). This could allow Mad Max a tax-free step-up in Edsel's assets.

Question 4. Can Mad Max apply Edsel's loss against its future income by purchasing at least 80% of Edsel's stock and filing a consolidated return?

Answer 4. No, not without limitation. Since Edsel was not a member of an affiliated group with Mad Max for the years in which the NOLs were created, these losses would be from separate return limitation years (SRLY losses). These would be limited by §1.150221(c) to the income of Edsel.

Note that the §382 limitations would also apply to a stock purchase and this limitation is in *addition* to the SRLY limitation.

Question 5. Would there be any benefit from filing consolidated returns if Mad Max is unable to offset Edsel's pre-acquisition losses against Mad Max's income?

Answer 5. If Edsel continues to operate at a loss, then filing a consolidated return would be beneficial since Mad Max could offset Edsel's post-acquisition losses against Mad Max's future income. Neither §382 nor the consolidated return rules apply to limit post-acquisition losses. Although it has been held in some cases that §269 can apply to limit benefit from post-acquisition losses of an acquired company, this is an unsettled area.

Question 6. Max thinks he can at least avoid the application of the SRLY rules by purchasing all of Edsel's stock and then liquidating Edsel. Will this work?

Answer 6. Mad Max could purchase at least 80% of Edsel's stock for cash and then liquidate Edsel under §332. Since a consolidated return requires at least two corporations, the SRLY limitation would not be a problem. However, the §382 limitations discussed previously *would apply* to the 80% stock purchase. Section 269(b) (discussed in Question 8) could also apply.

Question 7. Assume that Mad Max only wishes to purchase 51% of the stock of Edsel. To what extent would the limitations of §382 apply?

Answer 7. The rules of §382(b), as discussed in Question 3, apply to stock acquisitions of NOL companies involving a more than 50% ownership change. Since Mad Max is acquiring 51% of Edsel, the §382 rules apply to Edsel's NOL. However, unlike the situation in Question 5, Edsel and Mad Max are not eligible to file in the same consolidated tax return group. Only affiliated groups can elect to file consolidated tax returns and §1504 (defining affiliation) would require Mad Max to own at least 80% of Edsel.

Question 8. What other factors should be considered when acquiring a corporation with loss carryovers?

Answer 8. Section 269(a), in addition to §382, may be applied to an acquisition. This provision can apply if it can be shown that the "principal purpose" of the acquisition of Edsel is to evade or avoid federal income taxes. Mad Max must prove that there is a primary business purpose for the acquisition.

Arguably, the transaction is motivated principally by business reasons. For example, there would be a continuing business in the service and repair departments of Edsel. The operating assets, reputation, and the business location of Edsel would also be retained. The showroom of Edsel Record Players, Inc. furnishes another place of business for the display and sale of foreign compact disc players already marketed by Mad Max.

Thus, there are many business reasons that could defeat a tax-avoidance charge. However, in §269 litigation, the burden of proof is on the taxpayer, not the IRS.

Section 269(b) should also be considered. If 100% of Edsel stock is acquired in a taxable purchase, and Edsel is liquidated within two years (with no §338 election being made), the IRS could also attack the liquidation as being principally tax-motivated under §269(b). (Mad Max might liquidate Edsel to circumvent the SRLY restrictions as discussed earlier in Question 6.) Mad Max would probably have more difficulty in refuting an attack under §269(b), since he must prove the liquidation, and not the original acquisition, was principally motivated by business reasons.

Chapter 6

Taxable Acquisitions Involving Sole Proprietorships, S Corporations, Partnerships, and LLCs

Objectives

This chapter will explain the differing tax consequences and considerations related to taxable acquisitions of a business operated by a sole proprietorship, an S corporation, and a partnership.

Introduction

Up to this point, we have considered situations in which a business has been acquired by a corporate seller, with this seller operating in the form of a so called "C" or regular corporation. Of course, many businesses are operated in other entities. These can include an S corporation, partnership, limited liability company (LLC) or sole proprietorship. We will now examine special tax consequences when a business is acquired from such entities, building on the discussion contained in previous chapters.

Acquisitions from a Sole Proprietorship

The simplest case is the acquisition of a business operated as a sole proprietorship. Such an operation will typically be disclosed on the seller's federal income tax return on a Schedule C. The seller will compute gain or loss, using the purchase price allocation rules of §1060. Because the business is not operated in corporate form, there will be no imposition of double tax (any gain will be taxed only to the sole proprietor, as there is no other legal entity involved in the ownership of the business assets). Since no entity apart from the sole proprietor is involved, the acquisition can only be structured as the purchase of assets.

Acquisition of a Business from an S Corporation

There are special considerations involved when an S corporation is involved in an acquisition.

By way of review, an S corporation is one taxed under the special provisions of subchapter S of the Internal Revenue Code. Under current law an S corporation is a corporation that is, in many ways, treated like a partnership.

In the absence of a special election, a corporation would be treated as a "C" or regular corporation, the type of corporation discussed in the previous chapters. S corporation status must be elected by the shareholders and there are restrictions on corporations that can elect S corporation status. Some of the particular characteristics of S corporations will be alluded to in this book. However, time constraints do not permit a detailed discussion of all the tax rules relevant to S corporations.

Broadly speaking, a corporation can make the S election at the time of its formation. This is the simplest situation, since the corporation would be taxed under the S corporation rules from the start. A more complex possibility is the situation where a "C" or regular corporation elects S Corporation status after operating as a "C" corporation for some period of time. The period during which the corporation operates prior to electing S status can present some additional complexities. As discussed below, these can impact the tax consequences to an S corporation selling a business to a buyer.

Other considerations are that an S corporation cannot have certain types of taxpayers as shareholders (for example, retirement plans and §501(c)(3) organizations can be shareholders) without terminating the election and there is a limitation on the number of shareholders (i.e., 75 shareholders). The presence of ineligible shareholders (e.g., C corporations) or the existence of excess passive income can cause the S election to terminate, with adverse tax consequences to the S corporation shareholders.

In general, tax considerations when an S corporation is involved in an acquisition include the following:

- Whether the S election terminates because of the transaction, and

- The shareholders' other tax consequences in the transaction.

In a taxable acquisition involving an S corporation there are two potential alternative transactions:

- The purchase of the S corporation's assets; or

- The purchase of the S corporation's stock.

Taxable Acquisitions Involving Sole Proprietorships, S Corporations, Partnerships, and LLCs

We will now consider tax consequences involved in each of these alternatives.

Purchase of S Corporation's Assets

In this situation the S corporation is the target company whose assets are purchased. The purchase price allocation issues and other considerations discussed previously would apply. This means, for example, that the purchaser and the selling S corporation would be bound by the purchase price allocation rules of §1060 and the other tax law provisions impacting the seller's gain and loss, such as §1245. However, there are also other provisions that can apply when the seller is an S corporation.

Passive Income Limitation

The target S corporation's subchapter S election would not necessarily terminate if its assets are purchased by another taxpayer. However, the target S corporation subchapter S election could terminate if the S corporation was previously a C corporation with E&P (earnings and profits), and the cash proceeds from the asset sale are invested and generate excess passive income for three consecutive years [§1362(d)]. This potential problem could also arise if debt or stock given to the S corporation for its assets generate excessive passive income.

Example 6-1

X, an electing S corporation, sells all its assets to P for cash and invests the proceeds in stock and securities generating interest and dividends.

If X had been a regular C corporation with earnings and profits prior to electing S status, this passive income could cause its S corporation status to be jeopardized.

Gain on Asset Sale

Under the rules discussed earlier in the book, the S corporation assets' sale will create gain if the purchase price exceeds the assets' tax basis. However, absent §1374 complications, the recognized gain will flow through to the S corporation shareholders and increase the shareholders' basis in their stock, reducing any gain that would otherwise be recognized when the S corporation is liquidated. Thus, an important difference between a C corporation and an S corporation is that there is generally no double taxation when an S corporation sells its assets.

If a purchaser (P) acquires the S corporation's stock and makes no §338 election (discussed earlier in the book), the S corporation's shareholders recognize gain on the stock sale with no S corporation tax incurred. However, P receives no basis step-up in the S corporation assets.

Adviser's Guide to Tax Consequences of the Purchase and Sale of a Business

Because of these results, P will generally prefer to purchase the target S corporation's assets and receive a stepped-up asset basis. The S corporation shareholders (if properly advised) understand this fact, and generally expect a premium for structuring an asset versus a stock sale.

Given the premium and the one level of taxation, the S corporation shareholders also generally prefer an asset sale. Consequently, a taxable acquisition of the S corporation's assets is generally preferable (and more common) to the acquisition of its stock (discussed in the next section).

Example 6-2

P is considering the purchase of a business operated by T, an S corporation. The purchase of assets would result in increased depreciation/amortization for tax purposes.

Therefore, P would prefer the purchase of assets to a purchase of stock.

T's shareholders recognize this fact and negotiate for a premium in the purchase price (versus a stock sale), because P will have significant after-tax benefits from structuring the transaction in this fashion.

A Purchaser Acquires the S Corporation's Stock

Potential Termination of the S Election

If the target S corporation's stock is purchased, the restrictions on eligible S corporation shareholders should be carefully considered. If, for example, the acquisition is made by P (a C corporation), the S election will terminate (because a corporation is not an eligible S corporation shareholder). However, even if individual taxpayers acquire the S corporation stock, there may still be problems with ineligible shareholders or the number of shareholders exceeding 75.

Tax Impact

The target S corporation shareholders recognize a capital gain or loss on the sale of their stock based on their S corporation stock basis. If the target S corporation stock is not publicly traded, §453 installment sale treatment should be considered.

Example 6-3

P (a C corporation) wishes to acquire T, an electing S corporation.

However, P recognizes that its direct acquisition of T will cause T's S corporation status to terminate, which P does not desire.

> Consequently, it is proposed that P's shareholders, rather than P, acquire the stock of T.
>
> **Evaluating Shareholders**
>
> Although this structure may allow T's S election to continue, care should be taken in evaluating shareholders.
>
> If P has shareholders ineligible to be S corporation shareholders (e.g., an ineligible trust), the acquisition could still cause T's S election to terminate.
>
> This would also be the result if the number of P shareholders was in excess of the amount permitted for S corporation purposes.

Asset Versus Stock Sale

While the sale of assets would generally be preferable to an S corporation stock sale (as discussed previously), other considerations may suggest a stock sale. These include the following:

- Certain state taxes may be incurred in an asset sale that would not be incurred in a stock sale;

- The S corporation may have a low basis in its assets compared to its shareholder's stock basis; or

- The S corporation has built-in gains that would be taxed on an asset sale under Section 1374.

> ### Example 6-4
>
> Charlie, Inc. (Charlie), a C corporation that manufactures and sells kites, wants to acquire Brown, Inc. (Brown), an S corporation that grows and plants landscaping trees.
>
> **Charlie Favors Asset Purchase; Brown Favors Stock Sale**
>
> Charlie favors an asset purchase allowing it to step up Brown's asset tax basis.
>
> Brown, a former C corporation, has significant §1374 built-in gains and also has passive income.
>
> Brown also realizes that a stock sale would avoid state taxes.

> However, absent an unattractive §338 election, Charlie would not receive a stepped-up basis in Brown's assets.
>
> This example illustrates the differing tax concerns of the buyer and seller.

Acquisitions Involving Partnerships

An acquisition can sometimes involve the acquisition of a business by a partnership, or the acquisition of partnership assets or a partnership interest. The rest of this chapter is a discussion of some of the tax considerations related to these types of transactions.

This material will cover certain aspects of acquisitions that are unique to partnerships. However, a complete review of the intricacies of partnership taxation is beyond the scope of this book.

The rest of this chapter will specifically review the following as a means of acquiring a business operated by a partnership:

- The purchase of business assets from a partnership; and
- The purchase of an interest in a partnership.

Purchase of Assets from a Partnership

Consequences to the Selling Partnership

An acquisition may involve the purchase of some, or all, of the assets of a partnership. In this case gain or loss on the sale of assets would be computed at the partnership level. The allocation of the sale price to individual assets and computation of gain/loss would be computed under the rules discussed in Chapter 2, "Taxable Asset Transactions." The gain/loss would be allocated to the individual partners in accordance with the partnership agreement and the tax law.

The partnership would also have to insure that any necessary additional information filings with the IRS (e.g., §1060 reporting requirements) are made. The sale of all the assets of the partnership may be a prelude to the termination of the partnership. This would involve the distribution of all sale proceeds (less amounts used to satisfy liabilities) to the partners.

Consequences to the Purchaser

The purchase of partnership assets will result in the same consequences as the purchase of assets from another entity (e.g., from an individual or a corporation). For example, the basis and allocation rules discussed in Chapter 2 would apply to this type of transaction. The fact that the assets were purchased from a partnership would imply no special consequences to the purchaser.

Example 6-5

ABC Partnership sells assets to X, a corporation.

ABC will compute gain or loss on an asset-by-asset basis under the rules of §1060. This gain or loss will be allocated to the individual partners.

X will allocate basis to the acquired assets under the rules of §1060.

Purchase of a Partnership Interest

Instead of purchasing individual assets owned by a partnership, a purchaser may instead purchase an interest in the partnership. Rather than owning certain assets of the partnership outright, the buyer in this case would own an interest in the partnership, which in turn would own the individual assets. The tax considerations in this case are different from those in an outright purchase of assets. Keep in mind the acquisition of a partnership interest would give the purchaser an undivided interest in all the assets of the business, rather than 100% ownership of specific assets. If the buyer's intent is to acquire 100% of the business, 100% of the partnership interest would have to be purchased. This is discussed more fully below.

Consequences to the Seller of a Partnership Interest

Under §1001 the seller of a partnership interest would compute gain or loss on the sale as the difference between the sales price and the adjusted tax basis in the partnership interest.
We will first consider the proceeds the selling partner would be deemed to receive for the interest and then the tax basis the selling partner has in the interest. The difference between the two is the gain or loss recognized on the sale of the interest.

Sales Price

The sales price would be the sum of the following:

- The cash paid for the interest;

- The value of any noncash property given for the interest; and

- The selling partner's share of partnership liabilities assumed by the buyer.

This last item is deemed to be part of the sales price under §752 because the selling partner is deemed to receive compensation in being relieved of his share of partnership liabilities.

Adjusted Tax Basis in the Partnership Interest

Under §742 the starting point for determining the selling partner's adjusted tax basis is the original cost. This would include any purchase price paid for the interest, plus any liabilities assumed in acquiring the interest [§752].

However, the tax law provides that this original basis is adjusted for a variety of items [§705]. For example, distributions of cash to a partner will reduce the partner's basis in the partnership interest, while contributions of capital will increase the basis.

Also, the share of taxable income allocated to a partner will increase his basis, while the loss allocated to him will decrease his basis in the partnership. Therefore, the computation of a partner's gain or loss on the sale of his interest will require a determination of his initial basis plus any adjustments required by the tax law. Normally, the individual partners are responsible for the determination of their basis, because this is not a responsibility of the partnership.

Nature of Gain/Loss on the Sale of the Interest

Section 741 of the Internal Revenue Code indicates that, generally, a partnership interest is a capital asset and the gain/loss from the taxable disposition of such an asset will give rise to capital gain or capital loss.

Example 6-6a

X sells his interest in the ABC Partnership for $10,000.

His tax basis in the interest is $4,000.

His gain would be $6,000 and, subject to the rules discussed below, should be capital in nature.

Ordinary Income Under Section 751

While a partnership interest is generally a capital asset, ordinary income can be recognized by the seller under the provisions of §751. Section 751(a) mandates ordinary income, rather than capital gain treatment, for certain assets. These assets include "unrealized receivables" of the partnership and inventory that has appreciated substantially in value. See IRS Form 8308, "Report of a Sale or Exchange of Certain Partnership Interests," discussed in Chapter 7, "Federal Income Tax Reporting Requirements."

Under §751(c) unrealized receivables are those that would be ordinary income when recognized, but which have not been recognized under the partnership's method of accounting. The typical case is the value of accounts receivable from sales of inventory that have not been recognized for tax purposes because the partnership is on the cash method of accounting.

Also, it should be kept in mind that unrealized receivables include §1245 property and §1250 property, which potentially may generate substantial amounts of depreciation recapture, thus reducing or eliminating any capital gain therefrom.

Substantially appreciated inventory [§751(d)] is inventory with a fair market value that is greater than

- 120% of its adjusted tax basis; and
- 10% of the fair market value of all the partnership's assets (besides cash).

Example 6-6b

In the above example, if X's share of gain on unrealized receivables and substantially appreciated inventory was $2,000, then

- $2,000 of his gain would be ordinary income, and
- The remaining $4,000 would be capital gain.

Close of Tax Year with Respect to the Selling Partner

In the event that the sale of the partnership interest occurs during the tax year of the partnership, the partnership tax year closes with respect to the selling partner [§706(c)(2)]. This means that the selling partner will recognize his share of partnership income or loss through the date of sale [§706(d)].

However, under the rules for partnership accounting [§705], this recognized income (loss) will increase (decrease) his tax basis in the partnership interest and will impact the gain or loss on the sale.

Example 6-6c

Recognition of Income upon Sale

Returning to the previous example, assume the partnership has a December 31 year-end, and X sells his interest effective July 1.

> X will recognize the income or loss from partnership operations for the first six months of the year.
>
> Assume that this amounts to $3,000 of income.
>
> **Increase in Basis, Reduction in Gain**
>
> X will have to recognize this income, but it will increase his basis in his interest by $3,000.
>
> Therefore, his gain on the sale of his interest will be reduced by $3,000.

Sale of Partial Interest

The partnership year will close with respect to the selling partner only if his/her entire interest is sold. If, for example, a partner sells one-half of his/her interest, the tax year cutoff discussed above does not result [§706(c)(2)(b)].

Consequences to the Purchaser of a Partnership Interest

The purchaser of a partnership interest will have a tax basis in the interest equal to the price paid for the interest, plus the share of partnership liabilities he/she assumes as a partner, under the rules of §§742 and 752, discussed above.

Allocable Basis to the Purchasing Partner under Section 743(a)

There is a special consideration that can affect the purchasing partner's share of depreciation from the assets of the partnership. Normally, under §743(a), a partner will be entitled to a proportionate share of the assets of the partnership. This will be based on the historical basis of the partnership assets and will not reflect the price paid for the interest in the partnership. Specifically, §743(a) provides that "the basis of partnership property shall not be adjusted as the result of a transfer of an interest in the partnership by sale or exchange...."

> **Example 6-7a**
>
> A pays $5,000 for a one-third interest in the XYZ Partnership. At the time of purchase the partnership has no liabilities and its assets are all depreciable.
>
> **Adjusted Basis of Partnership's Assets**
>
> The adjusted tax basis of the partnership's assets is $9,000.

> **A's Share of Basis**
>
> Absent the special rules discussed below, A's allocable share of the asset basis (upon which his depreciation deduction will be computed) will be $3,000.
>
> This is despite the fact that he paid $5,000 for his interest.

Special Election Under Section 743(b)

However, a special provision of the tax law [§743(b)] allows the purchaser to translate the price paid for his/her interest into depreciable tax basis.

Provided that a special election under §754 is in effect, §743(b) permits the basis of partnership assets allocable to the new partner to be adjusted to reflect the price he/she paid for his interest.

For example, if the basis in his interest (computed under the rules discussed previously) is greater than his/her allocable basis in the partnership assets, §743(b) will increase the basis of partnership assets with respect to the new partner. Conversely, if the partner's basis in the partnership is less than his/her allocable share of asset basis, the basis of the assets will be reduced with respect to him.

> **Example 6-7b**
>
> Returning to Example 6-7a, assume that an election under §754 has been made by the partnership.
>
> In this case A's allocable share for depreciation purposes will be $5,000.
>
> This has the effect of increasing the deductions allocable to A by $2,000 over the tax life of the assets.

Tax Planning

Note that the adjustment under §743(b) only affects the new partner. It does not impact the basis allocable to the continuing partners. Many partnerships will ensure the §754 election is in effect (it must be made by the partnership, not by the individual partners). This will facilitate transfers of partnership interests and allow a purchasing partner to translate his purchase price into allocable depreciable basis.

Adjustment Rules of Section 755

In some cases the adjustment rules of §755 may prevent a "simple" translation of interest purchase price into allocable asset basis. A discussion of §755 is beyond the scope of this book, but it should be reviewed when a §743(b) adjustment is made as the result of the sale of a partnership interest.

Consequences to the Continuing Partners and the Partnership

If a purchaser only wanted to acquire a portion of the business of the partnership, the purchaser could acquire less than all of the available interests in the partnership. When a partner sells his/her interest in the partnership, the assets and liabilities of the partnership continue to be accounted for at the partnership level. Generally, there is no tax impact to the continuing partners (i.e., those partners who did not sell their interest).

An exception under §708 provides that if there is a sale or exchange of 50% or more of the interest in partnership capital and profits within a twelve-month period, the partnership is considered terminated for tax purposes. This results in a hypothetical distribution to the purchasing and continuing partners, who are then deemed to recontribute their assets to the partnership.

Principal Consequences

Consider the following.

Partnership Year-End

The partnership year ends for all partners, not only the partners who sell their interests. This can result in disadvantageous consequences to the partners if the partnership and its partners are on different tax years, due to a bunching of income.

Example 6-8

ABC Partnership has three partners, A, B, and C. The partners are on a December 31 year-end, while the partnership is on a September 30 year-end. The partnership has generated taxable income for several years.

Assume the partnership terminates on November 30, 2005, under §708 due to sale of A's 50% interest in the capital and profits of the partnership.

Analysis

The partnership tax rules normally provide that partnership profit and loss will be recognized by the partners in their tax year in which, or with which, the partnership year ends [§706(a)].

Taxable Acquisitions Involving Sole Proprietorships, S Corporations, Partnerships, and LLCs

> Therefore, the partnership income for the tax year from October 1, 2004, to September 30, 2005, will be reportable by the partners in their 2005 tax returns.
>
> Furthermore, the profit for the period from October 1, 2005, to November 30, 2005, will also be reportable by the partners on their 2005 tax returns (since the partnership is deemed to terminate due to the sale of A's interest).
>
> Thus, 14 months of partnership income will be reportable on the partners' 2005 tax returns.
>
> Note this is the case for B and C (as well as A), even though B and C did not sell their interests.

Consequences of Deemed Termination

- *Elections* – The elections made by the partnership are voided for tax purposes; new elections (dealing with such matters as method of accounting and the §754 election discussed earlier) must be made.

- *Gain/Loss Under §731* – If the cash deemed distributed to a partner because of the termination exceeds his basis in the partnership, gain will be recognized under §731 to the extent of this excess. Conversely, loss will be recognized if the amount of cash and the total of unrealized receivables and substantially appreciated inventory (discussed previously) are less than his interest in the partnership.

- *Basis of Assets* – Under §732 the total basis of the partnership assets will be equal to the total basis the partners have in their partnership interests; this implies that if the fair value of the assets exceeds the historical basis of the assets, the asset basis will be stepped up to fair market value.

Tax Planning Comment: Buy-Sell Agreements and Right of First Refusal

To prevent unintended tax consequences, and for other business reasons, partnership agreements often contain restrictions on the ability of partners to sell or otherwise transfer their partnership interests. These provisions will typically provide that before a partner can transfer his interest, it must be offered for sale to the partnership. This provision normally provides how the offering price will be determined. In some cases the agreement will provide that the partnership must be allowed to repurchase the partner's interest by matching a bona fide offer the partner has received from a third party (a *right of first refusal*).

Such arrangements (typically called *buy-sell agreements*) allow the partnership to exercise some control over who participates in the business, while giving a partner who wishes to leave the business some assurance that he will receive a fair price for his interest.

Limited Liability Companies

Background

A business entity that has been gaining in popularity is the Limited Liability Company or LLC. Essentially, this entity combines the limited liability of a corporation with the flow-through and other characteristics of a partnership. The LLC offers tax planners a combination of attributes that were not previously available in a single type of entity.

LLCs will generally be classified as partnerships for tax purposes. The effect of this is that they will typically avoid the two levels of taxation discussed previously in connection with the corporate form of business. However, unlike a partnership, members of an LLC do not have to concern themselves with the level of activity they have in the venture. Note this is not the case for Limited Partnerships in which the limited partners can forfeit their limited liability characterization by becoming too involved in the activities of the business.

There is another consideration in connection with LLCs and that is the treatment of the LLC under state law. State statutes with respect to LLCs have been characterized as either being "flexible" or "bullet-proof." The so-called bullet-proof statutes provide that the LLC is classified as a partnership for federal tax purposes. However, depending on the way in which the organization is designed, an LLC formed under a flexible state statute may not be classified as a partnership. In general, if the LLC's corporate documents do not indicate which tax classification is desired, the normal provisions of the statute will cause the LLC to be governed as a partnership. However, depending on the location of the LLC, specific state statutes should be checked.

The primary use of the LLC to this point has been for business activities that may have historically been undertaken in the partnership form and which involve a high degree of risk. An example would be oil and gas exploration activities. Another application would involve multinational operations. For example, countries apply different entity classification standards. Therefore, an LLC that is treated as a partnership in the United States could be taxed as a corporation in another country. The treatment of the LLC as a flow-through entity in the U.S. and as a corporation in another country permits various tax planning opportunities.

Partnerships have also been converted to LLCs. Revenue Ruling 95-37 addresses several issues in connection with this conversion. These include whether the converting partnership's tax year closes with respect to its partners, whether or not the LLC needs to obtain a new taxpayer identification number and other matters. However, the conversion of an existing partnership into an LLC is a complex transaction. The tax consequences should be carefully considered before such a conversion is made.

In summary, while state rules vary, the basic benefit of the LLC is to offer LLC members both pass-through tax treatment and limited liability.

Acquisition of a Business from a LLC

The utilization of LLCs in connection with the purchase or sale of a business can present a variety of consequences. For example, in a state with a bulletproof LLC statute, the LLC will be classified as a partnership for federal tax purposes.

The consequences of the purchase or sale of such an interest (or the assets of the LLC) should therefore largely be governed by the partnership rules discussed earlier in this chapter. However, an LLC formed under a flexible statute may or may not be classified as a partnership. This can have different consequences to the owners when the business is sold. State tax consequences should also be considered.

Summary

This chapter has covered tax aspects of acquisitions involving partnerships. We have seen that the purchase of assets from a sole proprietorship, an S corporation, a partnership, or an LLC presents no unique considerations.

The purchase of a partnership interest does introduce additional complexity. Some of the special considerations include the nature of the gain recognized by the selling partner, the basis taken by the purchasing taxpayer and consequences to the continuing partners. These considerations include the cutoff of the tax year that can be triggered by the sale.

Chapter 7

Federal Income Tax Reporting Requirements

Objective

The purpose of this chapter will be to review the federal income tax reporting requirements for the various types of acquisitions discussed in this book, including—

- *Asset purchases governed by the rules of §1060. These include asset acquisitions from a C corporation, S corporation, sole proprietorship, partnership or LLC*

- *Stock purchases, involving an election under §338*

- *Sale or exchanges of certain partnership interests*

This chapter also contains a discussion of disclosure requirements that can be required under the provisions of §382.

Asset Purchases

Asset purchases were discussed in Chapter 2, "Taxable Asset Transactions." The regulations under §1060 contain the reporting requirements for asset purchases. These reporting requirements apply whether the asset purchase is from a C corporation, S corporation, sole proprietorship, partnership or limited liability company (LLC).

Under current rules, the seller and the purchaser must each file asset acquisition statements on Form 8594, *Asset Acquisition Statement (Under Section 1060)*, with their income tax returns for the taxable year that includes the first date assets are sold pursuant to an "applicable asset acquisition" (as discussed in Chapter 2). The form must be filed when there is the transfer of assets constituting a trade or business and when the purchaser's basis in the assets is determined by the amount paid (e.g., a taxable purchase). A copy of Form 8594 is included at the end of Chapter 2.

Note. A Form 8594 is not required to be filed when partnership interest is purchased (as opposed to the purchase of the underlying assets of the partnership). If a partnership interest is acquired, special reporting requirements may apply (see discussion later in this chapter).

When an increase or decrease in consideration is taken into account after the close of the first taxable year that includes the first date assets are sold, the seller and the purchaser must each file a *supplemental* asset acquisition statement on Form 8594. This filing must be included with the income tax return for the taxable year in which the increase (or decrease) is properly taken into account. Parts I and III of the Form 8594 are required to be completed in this instance. The Form 8594 instructions and the applicable regulations indicate the procedures to be followed in allocating an increase or decease in consideration that occurs in a tax year after the year of the original sale.

Form 8594 also requires certain disclosures, such as whether the purchaser and seller provided for an allocation of the sales price in the sales contract or in another written document signed by both parties.

The form also requires disclosure of whether the purchaser acquired a license or covenant not to compete, or entered into a lease agreement, employment contract, management contract or similar arrangement with the seller (or certain parties related to the seller). If so, the specifics of such agreement or agreements must be disclosed in an attachment to Form 8594.

Failure to file the Form 8594 may subject the taxpayer to a penalty under the provisions of §§6721 through 6724.

Stock Purchases

Typically, there is no special reporting required when the stock of a corporation is purchased.

However, when a stock purchase is accompanied by an election under §338(g) or §338(h)(10), special reporting requirements do apply. In the event of such an election, Forms 8023 (*Elections Under Section 338 for Corporations Making Qualified Stock Purchases*) and Form 8883 (*Asset Allocation Statement Under Section 338*) must both be filed. A copy of these forms is included at the end of this chapter.

Form 8023

Form 8023 permits elections to be made under §338 for the target corporation if the purchasing corporation has made a "qualified stock purchase" as discussed in Chapter 4, "Taxable Stock Transactions."

Generally, a purchasing corporation must file Form 8023 for the target. If a §338(h)(10) election is made for a target, Form 8023 must be filed jointly by the purchasing corporation and the common parent of the selling consolidated group. Note that if the target is an S corporation, the §338(h)(10) election must be made by all of the shareholders of the target S corporation.

Federal Income Tax Reporting Requirements

Form 8023 must be filed by the 15th day of the 9th month after the acquisition date to make a §338 election for the target. The Form 8023 has special instructions that must be followed in the case of foreign targets or foreign purchasers. The signature requirements of Form 8023 should also be noted.

Form 8883

Form 8883 is a form that provides for the reporting of certain information that previously had been reported on the Form 8023. The purchasing corporation's statement (formerly section E of Form 8023) has been moved to Form 8883. The seller's statement (formerly section F of Form 8023) has also been moved to Form 8883. Form 8883 is filed with the old target's and new target's income tax return for the year that includes the acquisition date.

For both a §338(g) and §338(h)(10) election, the old and new target must file Form 8833. Generally, the Form 8883 is to be attached to the tax return on which the effects of the §338 deemed sale and purchase of the target's assets are required to be reported. There are different filing requirements for the target parent of a consolidated group, a member of such a group, a target S corporation or a foreign target corporation, and the filing requirements discussed in the instructions to the Form 8883 should be considered. Various other disclosures are required in Section IV of Form 8883.

If the amount allocated to any asset is increased or decreased after the year in which the deemed sale under §338 occurs, a taxpayer impacted by the change must complete Parts I, II, III, IV and VI of Form 8883. The Form 8883 must be attached to the income tax return for the year in which the increase or decease in allocated amount is taken into account.

Failure to file Form 8883 when required may subject a taxpayer to a penalty under the provisions of §§6721 through 6724.

Sale or Exchange of Certain Partnership Interests

Form 8308 (*Report of a Sale or Exchange of Certain Partnership Interests*) is filed by a partnership to report the sale or exchange by a partner of all or part of a partnership interest where any money or other property received in exchange for the interest is attributable to unrealized receivables or inventory items (i.e., where there has been a §751(a) exchange, as discussed in Chapter 6, "Taxable Acquisitions Involving Sole Proprietorships, S Corporations, Partnerships, and LLCs"). A partnership must file a separate Form 8308 for each §751(a) exchange for an interest in such partnership.

Form 8308 must be filed once the partnership has notice of the §751(a) exchange. The Form 8308 indicates when a partnership is deemed to have received notice for this purpose.

Generally, Form 8308 must be filed as an attachment to Form 1065 for the tax year of the partnership that includes the last day of the calendar year in which the §751(a) exchange took place. It is due at the time for filing the partnership return, including extensions. Penalties can be imposed for the late filing of the Form 8308, or for failure to furnish correct Forms 8308 to the transferor and transferee of the partnership interest.

A copy of Form 8308 is included at the end of the chapter.

Section 382 and Loss Corporation Information Disclosure

In Chapter 5, "Carryover of Tax Attributes," ownership changes under §382 were discussed. If an ownership change of a loss corporation occurs, certain disclosure requirements are applicable. A loss corporation is defined in §382(k)(1) as a corporation entitled to use a net operating loss carryover, or having a net operating loss for the tax year in which an ownership change occurs.

Specifically, a loss corporation must file a statement with its income tax return for each taxable year that it is a loss corporation in which an owner shift (as discussed in Chapter 5) occurs. This statement must

- Indicate whether any testing dates occurred during the taxable year;

- Identify each testing date, if any, on which an ownership change occurred;

- Identify the testing date, if any, that occurred during and closest to the end of each of the three-month periods ending on March 31, June 30, September 30 and December 31 during the taxable year, regardless of whether an ownership change occurred on the testing date;

- Identify each 5% shareholder on each such testing date;

- State the percentage ownership of the stock of the loss corporation for each 5% shareholder as of each such testing date and the increase, if any, in such ownership during the testing period; and

- Disclose the extent to which the loss corporation relied upon the presumptions regarding stock ownership under the applicable §382 regulations to determine whether an ownership change occurred on any identified testing date.

Note. Also that the regulations require that a loss corporation maintain whatever records are required to determine:

- The identity of its 5% shareholders,

- The percentage of its stock owned by each such 5% shareholder, and

- Whether the §382 limitation is applicable.

Federal Income Tax Reporting Requirements

IRS Forms 8308, 8023, and 8883

Federal Income Tax Reporting Requirements

Form 8308
(Rev. March 2000)
Department of the Treasury
Internal Revenue Service

Report of a Sale or Exchange of Certain Partnership Interests

▶ Please print or type.

OMB No. 1545-0941

| Name of partnership | Telephone number ( ) | Employer identification number |

Number, street, and room or suite no. If a P.O. box, see instructions.

City or town, state, and ZIP code

Part I — Transferor Information (Beneficial owner of the partnership interest immediately before the transfer of that interest)

| Name | Identifying number |

Number and street (including apt. no.)

City or town, state, and ZIP code

Notice to Transferors: *The information on this form has been supplied to the Internal Revenue Service. The transferor in a section 751(a) exchange is required to treat a portion of the gain realized from the exchange as ordinary income. For more details, see* **Pub. 541,** *Partnerships.*

Statement by Transferor: *The transferor in a section 751(a) exchange is required under Regulations section 1.751-1(a)(3) to attach a statement relating to the sale or exchange to his or her return. See* **Instructions to Transferors** *on page 2 for more details.*

Part II — Transferee Information (Beneficial owner of the partnership interest immediately after the transfer of that interest)

| Name | Identifying number |

Number and street (including apt. no.)

City or town, state, and ZIP code

Part III — Date of Sale or Exchange of Partnership Interest ▶ / /

Sign Here Only if You Are Filing This Form by Itself and Not With Form 1065 or Form 1065-B

Under penalties of perjury, I declare that I have examined this return, including accompanying attachments, and to the best of my knowledge and belief, it is true, correct, and complete.

▶ Signature of general partner or limited liability company member   ▶ Date

---

General Instructions

Section references are to the Internal Revenue Code unless otherwise noted.

Purpose of Form. Form 8308 is filed by a partnership to report the sale or exchange by a partner of all or part of a partnership interest where any money or other property received in exchange for the interest is attributable to unrealized receivables or inventory items (i.e., where there has been a section 751(a) exchange).

Who Must File. A partnership must file a separate Form 8308 for each section 751(a) exchange of an interest in such partnership. See Regulations section 1.6050K-1.

Note: *Form 8308 does not have to be filed if, under section 6045,* **Form 1099-B,** *Proceeds From Broker and Barter Exchange Transactions, is required to be filed with respect to the sale or exchange.*

A partnership must file Form 8308 once the partnership has notice of the section 751(a) exchange. The partnership has such notice when either:

1. The partnership receives written notification of the exchange from the transferor that includes the names and addresses of both parties to the exchange, the identifying numbers of the transferor and (if known) of the transferee, and the date of the exchange; or

2. The partnership has knowledge that there has been a transfer of a partnership interest and, at the time of the transfer, the partnership had any unrealized receivables or inventory items.

No returns or statements are required under section 6050K if the transfer was not a section 751(a) exchange. For example, a transfer which in its entirety constitutes a gift for Federal income tax purposes is not a section 751(a) exchange.

A partnership may rely on a written statement from the transferor that the transfer was not a section 751(a) exchange unless the partnership has knowledge to the contrary. If a partnership is in doubt whether partnership property constitutes unrealized receivables or inventory items or whether a transfer constitutes a section 751(a) exchange, the partnership may file Form 8308 to avoid the risk of incurring a penalty for failure to file.

When To File. Generally, file Form 8308 as an attachment to Form 1065 or Form 1065-B for the tax year of the partnership that includes the last day of the calendar year in which the section 751(a) exchange took place. Form 8308 is due at the time for filing the partnership return, including extensions.

If, however, a partnership is notified of a section 751(a) exchange after it has filed its partnership return, file Form 8308 separately, within 30 days of notification, with the service center where Form 1065 or Form 1065-B was filed.

Copies of Form 8308 To Be Furnished to Transferor and Transferee. All partnerships required to file Form 8308 must furnish a copy of the form to each transferor and transferee by January 31 of the year following the calendar year in which the section 751(a) exchange occurred or, if later, 30 days after the partnership has notice of the exchange.

If the partnership does not know the identity of the beneficial owner of an interest in the partnership, the record holder of the interest is treated as the transferor or transferee.

Cat. No. 62503I

Form **8308** (Rev. 3-2000)

7-9

Form 8308 (Rev. 3-2000) — Page 2

Note: *The transferor of the interest is required to notify the partnership of the exchange of the partnership interest unless, under section 6045, Form 1099-B is required to be filed.*

Form 8308 must generally be prepared prior to the time it must be attached to the partnership return and sent to the IRS. This will allow the timely furnishing of Forms 8308 to the transferor and transferee.

Instructions to Transferors

This form alerts transferors that they are required to treat a portion of the gain realized from a section 751(a) exchange as ordinary income. For more details, see Pub. 541.

Separate Statement Required by Transferor. For transfers of partnership interests after December 14, 1999, you as the transferor are required by Regulations section 1.751-1(a)(3) to attach a statement to your income tax return for the tax year of the sale or exchange with the following information:

1. The date of the sale or exchange.

2. The amount of any gain or loss attributable to the section 751 property.

3. The amount of any gain or loss attributable to capital gain or loss on the sale of the partnership interest.

⚠ *For transfers of partnership interests before December 15, 1999, see Form 8308 (Rev. December 1996) for the information required to be included in the transferor's statement.*

Instructions to Partnerships

Section 751(a) Exchange. A section 751(a) exchange occurs when money or any property is exchanged for all or part of a partnership interest that is attributable to unrealized receivables or inventory items. Generally, any sale or exchange of a partnership interest (or any portion) at a time when the partnership has any unrealized receivables or inventory items is a section 751(a) exchange.

Unrealized Receivables. Unrealized receivables, to the extent not previously includible in income under the partnership's accounting method, are any rights to payment for:

1. Goods delivered or to be delivered, to the extent that the payment would be treated as received for property other than a capital asset, and

2. Services rendered or to be rendered.

Unrealized receivables also include the amount of gain that would be ordinary income if any of the following types of partnership property were sold on the date of the section 751(a) exchange:

- Mining property (section 617(f)(2)).
- Stock in an interest charge domestic international sales corporation (section 992(a)).
- Farm recapture property or farm land (section 1252(a)).
- Franchises, trademarks, or trade names (section 1253(a)).
- Oil, gas, or geothermal property (section 1254).
- Stock of a controlled foreign corporation (section 1248).
- Section 1245 property.
- Section 1245 recovery property.
- Section 1250 property.
- Market discount bonds (section 1278).
- Short-term governmental obligations (section 1283).
- Other short-term obligations (section 1283(c)).

Inventory Items. Inventory items are not just stock in trade of the partnership. They also include:

- Any properties that would be included in inventory if on hand at the end of the tax year or that are held primarily for sale to customers in the normal course of business.
- Any asset that is not a capital asset or is not treated as a capital asset.
- Any other property held by the partnership that would be considered inventory if held by the transferor partner.
- Any trade receivables of accrual method partnerships.
- Any property held by the partnership that, if sold, would result in a gain taxable under section 1246(a) (relating to gain on foreign investment company stock).

Tiered Partnerships. In determining whether partnership property is an unrealized receivable or an inventory item, the partnership is treated as owning its proportionate share of the property of any other partnership in which it is a partner. See section 751(f).

Penalty for Late Filing of Correct Form 8308. A penalty may be imposed for failing to file each Form 8308 when due, including extensions. The penalty may also be imposed for failing to include all required information on Form 8308 or for furnishing incorrect information. The penalty is based on when the partnership files a correct Form 8308. Generally, the penalty is:

- $15 per Form 8308 if the partnership correctly files within 30 days of the due date.
- $50 per Form 8308 if the partnership files more than 30 days after the due date or does not file correct Forms 8308.

If the partnership intentionally disregards the requirement to report correct information, the penalty per Form 8308 is increased to $100.

The penalty will not apply to any failure that the partnership can show was due to reasonable cause and not willful neglect.

For more details, see sections 6721 and 6724.

Penalty for Failure To Furnish Correct Forms 8308 to Transferor and Transferee. A penalty of $50 may be imposed for each failure to furnish when due a copy of Form 8308 to either party to the exchange. The penalty may also be imposed for each failure to give the transferor or transferee all required information on each Form 8308 or for furnishing incorrect information. If the partnership intentionally disregards the requirement to report correct information, each $50 penalty is increased to $100. The penalty will not apply to any failure that the partnership can show was due to reasonable cause and not willful neglect. See sections 6722 and 6724 for more details.

Partnership Address. Include the suite, room, or other unit number after the street address. If the Post Office does not deliver mail to the street address and the partnership has a P.O. box, show the box number instead.

Paperwork Reduction Act Notice. We ask for the information on this form to carry out the Internal Revenue laws of the United States. You are required to give us the information. We need it to ensure that you are complying with these laws and to allow us to figure and collect the right amount of tax.

You are not required to provide the information requested on a form that is subject to the Paperwork Reduction Act unless the form displays a valid OMB control number. Books or records relating to a form or its instructions must be retained as long as their contents may become material in the administration of any Internal Revenue law. Generally, tax returns and return information are confidential, as required by section 6103.

The time needed to complete and file this form will vary depending on individual circumstances. The estimated average time is:

Recordkeeping . . . . 2 hr., 23 min.
Learning about the law or the form . . . 2 hr., 23 min.
Preparing and sending the form to the IRS . . . 2 hr., 32 min.

If you have comments concerning the accuracy of these time estimates or suggestions for making this form simpler, we would be happy to hear from you. See the Instructions for Form 1065 or Form 1065-B.

7-10

Federal Income Tax Reporting Requirements

Form 8023
(Rev. October 2002)
Department of the Treasury
Internal Revenue Service

Elections Under Section 338 for Corporations Making Qualified Stock Purchases

▶ See separate instructions.

OMB No. 1545-1428

Section A-1—Purchasing Corporation

1a Name and address of purchasing corporation	1b Employer identification number
	1c Tax year ending / 1d State or country of incorporation

Section A-2—Common Parent of the Purchasing Corporation

2a Name and address of common parent of purchasing corporation	2b Employer identification number
	2c Tax year ending / 2d State or country of incorporation

Section B—Target Corporation

3a Name and address of target corporation	3b Employer identification number
	3c Tax year ending / 3d State or country of incorporation

Section C—Common Parent of Selling Consolidated Group, Selling Affiliate, S Corporation Shareholder, or U.S. Shareholder

(Complete only for a section 338(h)(10) election or if target was a member of a consolidated group or a controlled foreign corporation (CFC) (or had been a CFC within the preceding five years).)

4a Name and address of common parent of the selling consolidated group, selling affiliate, U.S. shareholder(s) of foreign target corporation, or S corporation shareholder(s)	4b Identifying number(s)
	4c Tax year ending

Section D—General Information

5a Acquisition date

5b What percentage of target corporation stock was purchased:
    (i) During the 12-month acquisition period? _____ %
    (ii) On the acquisition date? _____ %

For Paperwork Reduction Act Notice, see separate instructions.   Cat. No. 49972Z   Form **8023** (Rev. 10-2002)

Federal Income Tax Reporting Requirements

Form 8883
(October 2002)
Department of the Treasury
Internal Revenue Service

Asset Allocation Statement
Under Section 338

▶ Attach to your income tax return. ▶ See separate instructions.

OMB No. 1545-1806

Part I — Filer's Identifying Information

1a Name as shown on return

1b Identifying number as shown on return

1c Check applicable box (see instructions):
☐ Old target ☐ New target

1d Was a valid and timely Form 8023 filed? ☐ Yes ☐ No
If yes, enter the date filed ▶

Part II — Other Party's Identifying Information

2a Name of other party to the transaction

2b Other party's identifying number

Address (number, street, and room or suite no.)

City or town, state, and ZIP code

Part III — Target Corporation's Identifying Information

3a Name and address of target corporation

3b Employer identification number

3c State or country of incorporation

Part IV — General Information

4a Acquisition date

4b What percentage of target corporation stock was purchased:
  (i) During the 12-month acquisition period? _____ %
  (ii) On the acquisition date? _____ %

5a Stock price $

5b Acquisition costs/Selling costs $

5c Target liabilities $

5d AGUB/ADSP $

		Yes	No
6	Was the filer listed in Part I, above, a member of an affiliated group of corporations before the acquisition date?		
7	Was the target corporation a member of an affiliated group before the acquisition date?		
8	Is the target corporation or any target affiliate:		
a	A controlled foreign corporation? If "No," check here if it was a CFC at any time during the preceding 5 years ▶ ☐		
b	A foreign corporation with income, gain, or loss effectively connected with the conduct of a trade or business within the United States (including U.S. real property interests)?		
c	A qualifying foreign target under Regulations section 1.338-2(e)(1)(iii)?		
d	A corporation to which section 936 applies?		
e	A corporation electing under section 1504(d) or section 953(d)?		
f	A domestic international sales corporation (DISC)?		
g	A passive foreign investment company (PFIC)?		
h	If the answer to item 8g is "Yes", is the PFIC a pedigreed qualified electing fund?		

For Paperwork Reduction Act Notice, see separate instructions. Cat. No. 33707Y Form **8883** (10-2002)

Form 8883 (10-2002) Page **2**

Part V — Original Statement of Assets Transferred

9 Assets	Aggregate fair market value (actual amount for Class I)	Allocation of AGUB or ADSP
Class I	$	$
Class II	$	$
Class III	$	$
Class IV	$	$
Class V	$	$
Class VI and VII	$	$
Total	$	$

Part VI — Supplemental Statement of Assets Transferred

Complete if amending an original statement or previously filed supplemental statement because of an increase or decrease in AGUB or ADSP.

10 Enter the tax year and tax return form number with which the original Form 8023 or Form 8883 and any supplemental statements were filed.

11 Assets	Allocation of sales price as previously reported	Increase or (decrease)	Redetermined allocation of AGUB or ADSP
Class I	$	$	$
Class II	$	$	$
Class III	$	$	$
Class IV	$	$	$
Class V	$	$	$
Class VI and VII	$	$	$
Total	$		$

12 Reason(s) for increase or decrease. Attach additional sheets if more space is needed.

Form **8883** (10-2002)

Chapter 8

Other Acquisition-Related Issues

Objectives

The purpose of this chapter is to—

- *Explain the tax treatment of acquisition-related expenses; and*
- *Explain the tax considerations related to "golden parachute" and "greenmail" payments.*

Introduction

This chapter will provide a discussion of other issues that arise in the context of an acquisition. Specifically, it will address the tax aspects of the following:

- Fees and other expenses incurred in connection with the acquisition; and
- Compensation issues (specifically, golden parachute and greenmail payments).

Treatment of Expenses Incurred in an Acquisition

Expenses incurred in completing an acquisition are often considerable. These can include the following:

- Investment banking fees,
- Attorneys' fees,
- Accountants' fees, and
- Commitment fees.

Expensing vs. Capitalizing

A purchaser will typically attempt to expense as much of these costs as possible to increase the after-tax return from the acquisition. Taxpayers have taken the position that these expenses are, in some cases, deductible under §212 as expenses for the production of income or under §162 as ordinary and necessary business expenses.

The alternative to expensing these costs is to capitalize them. However, this treatment will not be as advantageous to the purchaser, particularly in a stock purchase:

- In the event of a stock purchase, these costs would be capitalized as additional tax basis in the stock. Absent a §338 election, this would result in no continuing tax deductions to the purchaser.

- In the event of an asset purchase (or a §338 election), the costs could partially be allocated to assets, which could generate no immediate tax deductions to the purchaser.

The following example illustrates the issues.

Example 8-1

P Corporation has acquired T and incurred significant acquisition expenses. The acquisition was structured as a stock purchase.

The acquisition expenses incurred by P included a large fee paid to the investment banking firm that arranged for the financing of the acquisition (a percentage of the acquisition price).

Other fees included fees paid to two law firms involved in the drafting of the acquisition documents and accounting fees paid to the accounting firm that reviewed various financial statements prepared in connection with the acquisition.

Must P Capitalize Its Expenses?

Since the acquisition was structured as a stock purchase, these fees will be capitalized as stock basis unless P can develop a position for either immediately expensing a portion of the costs incurred or allocating a portion of the fees in a way that will yield amortization deductions.

Takeovers: The Target's Tax Treatment

Generally, costs incurred in a *friendly* takeover must be capitalized (see later discussion in this chapter of the *Indopco* case). However, in an age of unfriendly (hostile) takeovers, a related issue involves the treatment of expenses incurred in resisting a takeover. A target company would want to deduct the costs incurred to prevent its takeover. The deduction was typically claimed under §162 as an expense necessary to protect the ongoing business activities of the corporation and/or to preserve shareholder wealth. (See discussion of *A.E. Staley Manufacturing Co.* below.)

Position of the Courts

The courts have applied the "origin of the claims" test in this area. This standard was adopted by the U.S. Supreme Court when it rejected the "primary purpose" test.

Under the latter test the determination of whether acquisition costs should be capitalized or expensed depended on the primary purpose for the expenses. This involved a determination of the purpose(s) for the expenditures and which was the most important. The Supreme Court held that such a standard required a facts and circumstances determination that was ambiguous and difficult to apply. The Court instead adopted the origin of the claim doctrine.

Under this standard the tax treatment of an expense would depend on the type of transaction that gave rise to it (i.e., the transaction that was the original purpose for the expenditure). This standard, which has application outside the area of acquisitions, has frequently been adopted by the courts in determining the proper treatment of acquisition expenses. This has usually resulted in acquisition expenses being capitalized more frequently than when the primary purpose test was applied.

In *Indopco* (92-1 USTC, para. 50,113) the Supreme Court ruled that various expenses incurred by the target (acquired) corporation in a friendly takeover were not deductible. The court rejected the concept that only expenditures that create a separate and distinct asset need be capitalized. The court clarified that in this area deductions are an exception to the general rule of capitalization.

In *A.E. Staley Manufacturing Co.* (TC, CCH Dec. 50,882, para. 48,309) the Tax Court held that investment bankers' fees and other costs incurred by a company in defending itself against a hostile (and ultimately successful) takeover attempt were nondeductible capital expenditures. The company argued (unsuccessfully) that since the takeover was hostile, this case was distinguishable from the Supreme Court's decision in *Indopco*.

However, the Court of Appeals for the Seventh Circuit overturned the Tax Court decision in *Staley*. The Court of Appeals allowed the deduction of some of the target corporation's expenses related to its attempt to defend against the takeover as a cost of defending the business. The court reasoned this issue was not specifically addressed by *Indopco*. However, the Court of Appeals still required the target to capitalize certain fees paid to investment bankers and for certain other services. The court held that these services helped to implement a capital transaction and the Supreme Court decision in *Indopco* would require these costs to be capitalized.

In *Wells Fargo v. Comm.* (86 AFTR 2d 2000-5815, 224 F3d 874, 2000-2 USTC, para. 50697), the Eighth Circuit held that the Indopco decision did not require certain due diligence and investigation costs in a friendly takeover to be capitalized. The court held that these expenses were incurred before the taxpayer decided to enter into the transaction and were therefore deductible by the target. The decision in this case provides a methodology for determining whether transaction related costs should be capitalized or expensed.

Position of the IRS

The IRS has generally taken a position that acquisition expenses are usually not an item of expense for tax purposes, but rather should be capitalized by the purchaser. The IRS has also addressed the treatment of expenses incurred by targets in resisting takeovers, and has suggested that generally these must also be capitalized.

In Letter Ruling 9144042 the IRS addressed the tax treatment of expenses incurred by both a target and a purchaser. In the situation addressed in the ruling, a target company (A) received an unsolicited acquisition offer from another corporation (X). The target decided to resist the takeover attempt and implemented several financial and legal actions to foil the takeover attempt.

As part of a negotiated settlement, A agreed to repurchase its shares, which had been acquired by X, and to pay certain expenses incurred by X's parent in connection with the attempted acquisition. The parties also agreed to refrain from any further takeover attempts.

Corporation A argued that the expenses it incurred should be deductible as ordinary and necessary business expenses under §162. Its position was that the actions it took were necessary to protect the shareholder wealth embodied in the ongoing business activity of A.

However, the IRS took the position that the expenses incurred to repurchase the A stock were capital in nature and resulted simply in an altered capital structure for A. Furthermore, since the payments made to X's parent were contained in the same settlement agreement and originated in the stock repurchase transaction (which was capital in nature), these payments also had to be capitalized.

In this ruling the IRS also indicated that fees and expenses incurred in an unsuccessful takeover attempt should be allocated based on the nature of the specific services performed. The question is whether any long-term benefit inured to the corporation as a result of the fees incurred.

In Revenue Ruling 73-580, the IRS took a position that could have a potentially serious impact on a company that is actively engaged in acquisitions. In this ruling the IRS maintained that a portion of the compensation expense incurred by a company for in-house legal and accounting personnel should be treated as an acquisition cost, rather than deducted as a §162 expense. The allocation would be made on the basis of the relative amount of time spent by the personnel on acquisitions (e.g., due diligence reviews) versus performing their normal duties. This could have the impact of requiring significant additional allocations to stock basis and/or goodwill.

Other Acquisition-Related Issues

It is doubtful that most taxpayers have historically followed the guidance provided in this ruling. Also, the allocation concept of the ruling has apparently not been uniformly enforced by the IRS. However, this issue has been raised in audits of acquisition-oriented companies.

The IRS has also issued proposed regulations (Prop. Reg. 1.263(a)-4), which will become effective upon their adoption. These regulations would require certain transaction costs incurred to acquire, create, or enhance intangible assets to be capitalized. These rules are subject to certain exceptions, safe harbors, and *de minimis* rules.

Tax Planning Comment

As a result of various court decisions and IRS rulings, taxpayers should carefully review fees and professional expenses incurred in an acquisition. To the extent a taxpayer cannot make a case for current deductibility, the IRS, on audit, can require the expenses to be capitalized.

Returning to Example 8-1, if debt was incurred in connection with the acquisition, P may be able to argue that a portion of the fees were related to the debt financing and then amortize this portion over the life of the debt.

P may also explore ways to write off a portion of the legal and accounting fees in the year of acquisition under §162 (as an ordinary and necessary expense). It will be important to have detailed invoices indicating the specific services performed and the amount charged for each of the services.

Although the uncertainty in this area was reduced somewhat by the Wells Fargo decision referred to above, ambiguities still remain. Taxpayers should carefully evaluate their expenditures in light of the current judicial and IRS guidance.

In the case of a stock purchase that is not accompanied by a §338 election, this means that no depreciable/amortizable tax basis will result. Instead, the expenses will have to be capitalized as stock basis.

Compensation Issues

Two costs often incurred in connection with acquisitions are *golden parachute* payments and *greenmail* payments:

- **Golden parachute payments** are certain "excess" payments made to executives of the target corporation that become payable to the executives in the event of a change in control of the company (i.e., a takeover).

- **Greenmail payments** are payments made to a corporate raider (acquirer) to redeem his stock in a target corporation, and/or to obtain his/her consent to refrain from further acquisition efforts.

The current tax consequences of these payments are discussed further below.

Golden Parachute Payments

"Excess parachute payments" made to certain designated "disqualified individuals" are not deductible by the paying corporation. Furthermore, any contract established before that date is subject to these rules if it is subsequently amended in a significant way.

Another punitive provision of the tax law (§4999) provides that individuals receiving such payments are subjected to a nondeductible 20% excise tax on the payments, in addition to the normal income tax payable.

The focus of §280G is on excess parachute payments. This is defined as the excess of the total parachute payment over the determined "base amount."

Application of Section 280G

There are a number of requirements for the golden parachute provisions of §280G to be applicable:

- The payments must be made to "disqualified individuals."

  Disqualified individuals are designated in §280G(c) to include the following:

  – An officer, shareholder, or highly compensated individual; and

  – An employee, independent contractor, or other specified individual (designated in the regulations under §280G) who performs services for the payor corporation.

- The payment must be a payment contingent on a change in ownership or control of the payor corporation and must exceed a certain threshold amount. Specifically, a parachute payment is defined in §280G(b)(2)(a) to be a compensation payment:

  – That is dependent on the change in ownership (or control) of the corporation, or in the ownership of a substantial portion of its assets; and

  – The present value of which is in total equal to or greater than three times the base amount.

  – The "base amount" is the individual's annualized compensation for the five most recent tax years ending before the date on which the change in control or ownership occurred. If the disqualified individual was not an employee or independent contractor of the corporation for this entire five-year period, the individual's base period is the portion of the five-year period during which the individual performed personal services for the corporation.

Determining Whether an Excess Parachute Payment Has Occurred

To summarize, there is a three-step process involved in determining if a parachute payment has occurred. Those steps are as follows:

1. Determine if the payment in question has been made to the type of disqualified individual specified in the Internal Revenue Code; if not, §280G is not applicable.

2. If the payment is made to a disqualified individual, determine whether it was triggered by the type of control or ownership change envisioned in §280G; if not, §280G is not applicable.

3. If the payment was made to a disqualified individual because of a change in ownership or control, determine if the payment is a parachute payment.

For condition (3) to be satisfied, the total present value of the contingent payments must exceed three times the base amount. A discount rate specified under the §280G regulations is used to determine the present value of payments to be made in the future (e.g., over a 24-month period beginning with the date the ownership change occurs). This provision was included in the law because frequently the entire parachute payment is not made at the day of change. Rather, all or a portion of it is payable at some future date(s).

Example 8-2a

Joe Evans has been employed by Alright Corporation since January 1, 2003. In 2004 Evans entered into an agreement with Alright under which he will receive a special payment of $300,000 in the event that control of the corporation changes hands.

In 2003 and 2004 Evans received an annual salary of $90,000 and $100,000, respectively. His base amount is the average of these two years (since he has worked less than five years) and equals $95,000 (($90,000 + $100,000)/2).

On January 1, 2005, Alright is taken over by foreign investors and the payment is made to Evans on that date under the terms of his agreement.

Result

Because $300,000 exceeds three times the base amount of $95,000, a parachute payment is deemed to have been made.

> **Example 8-2b**
>
> Assume in the above example that Evans's base amount is $110,000.
>
> **Result**
>
> In this case the payment is less than three times the base amount and the payment is not deemed to be a parachute payment.

Computation of the "Excess" Parachute Payment

Note that when the three conditions discussed above are satisfied, it is still necessary to determine the "excess" portion of a payment. It is the excess portion that is subject to the special tax treatment.

This is determined under the following formula, which allocates a portion of the individual's base amount against each of the payments:

$$\text{Allocable base} = \frac{\text{Present value of payment}}{\text{Total present value of all payments}} \times \text{base}$$

Note that if a single parachute payment is made, the present value of this payment will be reduced by the total base amount to determine the excess parachute payment.

> **Example 8-3a**
>
> Martha Stevens is a disqualified individual with a base amount of $100,000, who is entitled to receive two parachute payments, one of $200,000 and another of $400,000.
>
> The $200,000 payment is made at the time of the change in ownership or control, and the $400,000 is to be made at a future date.
>
> **Applying the Formula**
>
> Assume the present value of the $400,000 payment is $300,000 on the date of change in ownership or control.
>
> Thus, the total present value of the parachute payments is $500,000 ($200,000 + $300,000).
>
> The portions of the base amount allocated to these payments are $40,000 and $60,000, respectively, computed as follows:

> $$\frac{\$200,000}{\$500,000} \times \$100,000 = \$40,000$$
>
> $$\frac{\$300,000}{\$500,000} \times \$100,000 = \$60,000$$
>
> Thus, the amount of the first excess parachute payment is $160,000 ($200,000 - $40,000) and that of the second is $340,000 ($400,000 - $60,000).
>
> **Tax Consequence**
>
> It is the amount of the excess parachute payment that is not deductible by the payor corporation and is subject to a 20% excise tax under §4999.

Reduction for Reasonable Compensation

The amount of any excess parachute payment determined under the above rules can be reduced by an amount that the taxpayer can prove is "reasonable compensation" for services actually rendered by the disqualified individual. Further, the excess parachute amount can be further reduced by an amount that the taxpayer can prove is for services to be rendered on or after the change of ownership or control.

> **Example 8-3b**
>
> In the situation of Example 8-3a the amount of the excess parachute payment could be reduced to the extent the taxpayer could prove that all or a portion of the excess parachute payments were for services rendered prior to the change in control or ownership, or for services to be rendered after that date.

Tax Planning

As a practical matter, it is difficult to reduce excess parachute treatment by arguing that all or a portion of the excess amount represents reasonable compensation:

- It must be kept in mind that the burden of proof is clearly on the taxpayer in establishing a reasonable compensation argument.

- Maintaining that a portion of the excess represents compensation for past services requires the taxpayer to argue that the executive was under-compensated prior to the change in ownership or control. This is usually a difficult argument to make.

- It is frequently the case that executives of the target will not be retained by the acquiring company. Thus, it may not be feasible to argue that all or a portion of the excess payment is reasonable compensation for services to be performed after the change in ownership or control.

Tax Planning Comment: Exceptions to Golden Parachute Rules

Certain exceptions to the golden parachute rules are provided under §280G(b)(5). These include an exception for payments made by a "small business corporation" as defined under §1361(b) and for payments by certain closely held corporations where shareholder approval is obtained for the payments.

Greenmail Payments

These payments (a play on words, meaning the financial equivalent of blackmail) were typically made by a corporation to redeem its stock from a corporate raider who threatened to acquire control of the company.

The redemption price paid by a corporation for its stock is deductible. However, in the case of redemption from a corporate raider, the corporation often paid a premium to regain its stock. Some taxpayers took the position that this premium amount was deductible.

Also, "standstill agreements" were often entered into by the raider in consideration for the price paid for the stock. Under these agreements the raider would agree not to acquire (directly or indirectly) additional shares of target company stock for a specified period of time.

Example 8-4a

A Acquires Stock in X

A is a well-known corporate raider who has acquired control of several corporations in hostile takeovers.
A acquires a 15% interest in X corporation between August 1998 and January 1999.

The value of X's stock is currently $20 a share.

A threatens to make a public tender offer for the stock of X.

X Responds

On February 1, 1999, to reacquire (redeem) the stock held by A, X offers him $25 a share, a $5 per share premium above current market value. The offer is not made to other continuing shareholders of X.

Other Acquisition-Related Issues

> **A Executes Standstill Agreement**
>
> In connection with the redemption, A also executes a standstill agreement, under which he agrees not to reacquire any additional shares of X stock for a period of five years.
>
> X could not deduct any portion of the payments made to A [§162(k)].

Excise Tax Imposed on the Recipient

Further, §5881 provides that a recipient of such a payment is subject to a nondeductible 50% excise tax on the payment. While §162(k) does not define greenmail payments (it simply addresses redemption expenses), §5881 contains a definition of greenmail payments that will be subjected to the excise tax.

Specifically, §5881(b) defines greenmail to be any consideration transferred by a corporation to acquire (directly or indirectly) stock of the corporation from any shareholder if

- The shareholder held the stock for less than two years before entering into the agreement to make the transfer;

- At some time during the two-year period ending on the date of such acquisition, the shareholder, a person with a defined relationship to the shareholder or someone acting in concert with the shareholder makes (or threatens to make) a public tender offer for the stock of the corporation; and

- The acquisition was pursuant to an offer that was not made on the same terms to all shareholders.

The 50% excise tax imposed by §5881 is generally imposed on greenmail payments after December 22, 1987 (certain transitional rules were provided).

> **Example 8-4b**
>
> Returning to Example 8-4a, the conditions specified in §5881 are all satisfied.
>
> In this event A would be taxed on the gain he realized from the greenmail payment.
>
> His gain would be the difference between the $25 per share he receives for the stock and the price he paid for the stock.
>
> His excise tax would be 50% of the gain computed and would be in addition to the income tax due on the gain.

As can be seen, this provision has reduced the after-tax proceeds from greenmail payments and, along with other market-based factors, has probably been responsible for the reduction in the frequency and amount of greenmail payments.

Summary

In this chapter we have seen the issues involved in the tax treatment of fees and other expenses related to an acquisition. Ideally, a taxpayer will be able to argue that some portion of these costs can be expensed currently. The alternative is to have these costs capitalized. Unfortunately, this capitalization typically yields no tax benefit to the taxpayer.

The treatment of such expenses has been an area of increasing IRS scrutiny in recent years. The courts have adopted the "origin of the claims" test in evaluating the proper treatment of such expenses and this has generally made it more difficult to avoid capitalization.

Another concept addressed in this chapter was certain types of compensation payments sometimes made in connection with acquisitions. These include golden parachute payments and greenmail payments. The tax law now provides that excess parachute payments and greenmail payments are not deductible by the corporation making the payments. Further, excise taxes are now imposed on the recipient of such payments, in addition to the normal income tax liability.

Chapter 9

Ethical Focus: Taxation

Ethics Overview

Compliance with ethical and professional standards is at the very heart of what it means to be a CPA. Our profession was founded on the qualities of honesty, trustworthiness, being free of conflicts, doing what is right, and having due and proper support for our work and opinions. The need for all of us to uphold these values is just as true today as it was over 100 years ago, when CPAs first became a key part of the financial reporting process. Ethical compliance is, however, not just a luxury afforded to us. In the current environment of expanded responsibilities and transparency, greater liability, and new civil and criminal penalties for failure to meet professional standards, each of us is personally and professionally obligated to know and understand our ethical duties. The AICPA and state societies are committed to increasing awareness of ethical issues among our membership and assisting professionals in implementing the high ideals of our profession.

In November 2003, the Tax Section of the AICPA issued a strategic plan that cited three critical issues that had to be addressed for the membership to effectively serve the public interest. One of the three issues: ensuring that the members follow the highest ethical standards of tax practice. To address this issue, the Tax Section established two goals: restore respect for the profession through consistent communication, and maintaining and enforcing the highest ethical standards. The Tax Section adopted several action plans to pursue these goals, including educating members on tax ethical standards, communicating these standards to the membership and stakeholders such as government and the public, and developing and maintaining the highest tax ethical standards to make CPAs the most trusted tax advisors. One additional critical action plan: to re-establish and enhance the public perception of the Tax Section's objectivity. As tax practitioners know, each wave of new negative publicity about deemed abusive tax shelters and tax avoidance schemes makes it that much more important for each of us to honor and support our ethical standards. Let us briefly review a few of the more common ethical dilemmas and judgment calls you may run into in the course of your practice.

Key Ethical Dilemmas and Judgment Calls

Corporations, Partnerships, and LLCs

- Disguised sale or distribution? Capitalization or expense? Entity or disregarded entity?

- How buy-sell agreements may not meet the *bona fide* business arrangement requirement.

- How should series LLCs be taxed? What about intellectual property holding companies?

Small Businesses, S Corporations, and ESOPs

- Special expense issues and substantiation—does deductibility match up revenues to expenses?

- Compensation—underreported? Too low in S corporation? What about distributions?

- Valuation and financing of the ESOP transaction—inherent conflicts?

Estates, FLPs, and Charitable Trusts

- Use of revocable and irrevocable trusts and intra-family property transfers to preserve wealth—when do we overreach?

- What is the charitable deduction—and how is it valued?

- Jeopardizing the FLP or private foundation through self-dealing and investments

NPOs

- How do I handle unrelated business income? Excess benefits? What about lobbying costs?

- Will this expose the organization to intermediate sanctions?

- Using for-profit subsidiaries and joint ventures—how much is too much?

Employee Benefit Programs

- Limit violations—will the plan qualify? How do I handle confidential disclosure issues?

Individual

- Return disclosure rules—what can I tell third parties?

- When does saving taxes become tax avoidance? What should my response be?

Addressing Ethical Dilemmas

When you encounter an ethical dilemma in rendering tax services, bear in mind the following professional conduct principles, among the most important in our profession. The citations are to provisions of the *Code of Professional Conduct*. You can access the complete *AICPA Code of Professional Conduct* at www.aicpa.org/about/code/index.htm.

- "Members should accept the obligation to act in a way that will serve the public interest…" Be "guided by the precept that when members fulfill their responsibility to the public, clients' and employers' interests are best served." [§53, Article II.02]

- "Integrity can accommodate the inadvertent error and the honest difference of opinion; it cannot accommodate deceit or subordination of principle." [§54, Article III.03]

- "Members employed by others to prepare financial statements or to perform auditing, tax or consulting services are charged with the same responsibility for objectivity as members in public practice…" [§55, Article IV.04]

Available Resources

Accounting professionals have a multitude of resources available to provide guidance on ethical issues. In addition to the *Code of Professional Responsibility* and the *Interpretations and Ethics Rulings* under the Code, each state has its own Code that has been adopted by the state society or state accountancy board. Many states maintain ethics hot lines staffed by knowledgeable CPAs who are trained to give you advice on how to handle specific ethical issues. Further guidance is available from rules adopted by the Securities and Exchange Commission, the Service (under the Code and Circular 230), and other government regulatory agencies.

The AICPA recently introduced a new CPE course designed to explore common ethical issues encountered by accounting professionals. Entitled *"Real World Business Ethics: How Will You React?,"* this program features true-to-life cases involving topical ethical issues—set in the context of audits, forensic investigations, tax and consulting services, as well as management reporting and disclosure. If you are looking for an up-to-date ethics refresher in an interactive, case-based setting, we encourage you to contact your state society to find out when they will be offering this course. You can also access individual case studies from this course through AICPA Infobytes. Each individual case study carries one hour of CPE ethics credit and asks you to address an ethical dilemma you face in various positions, such as the engagement partner, review partner, CFO, corporate controller, and forensic investigator. These case studies are at www.cpa2biz.com/OnlineProducts/AICPA+InfoBytes/Ethics/default.htm.

The AICPA's Professional Ethics Division also has an abundant range of information available for members at www.aicpa.org/members/div/ethics/index.htm, including fact sheets and other resources, ethics exam materials, and current developments in ethics such as rule updates, exposure drafts and comment letters. Through the Division's Web page, you can hyperlink to Infobyte CPE courses on independence, professional ethics, and selected ethics topics, and get information about how to contact the AICPA Ethics Hotline by phone (888-777-7077, followed by menu options 5 and 2) or by e-mail (ethics@aicpa.org). You can hyperlink from the Division's Web page to review changes to independence and other standards, as well as implementation guidelines for these standards, adopted under the Sarbanes-Oxley Act of 2002. You can also search for ethics articles published in the *Journal of Accountancy* and *The CPA Letter* through the AICPA Web site.

The Professional Ethics Division's Web page also has a link to the Statements on Standards for Tax Services (SSTSs) that, when opened, provides links to a variety of other tax-related resources, including the Tax Section's Strategic Plan Proposal, practice guides, updates on new and proposed rules, content and analysis of the SSTSs, and the latest data on abusive shelters and expanding shelter definitions.

Legislative Developments

On October 4, 2004, President Bush signed the Working Families Tax Relief Act of 2004 (WFTRA). The tax reductions provided consist mainly of the extension of certain tax breaks scheduled to expire, delays in the reduction of other tax breaks, and the acceleration of certain phase-ins previously scheduled for later years.

On October 22, 2004, President Bush signed the American Jobs Creation Act of 2004 (AJCA). This act changes the taxation of foreign business income and provides incentives for manufacturers, as well as other provisions affecting individuals and businesses, particularly S corporations.

See Appendix B, "Summary of Provisions of The Working Families Tax Relief Act of 2004 and the American Jobs Creation Act of 2004," for a brief explanation of the pertinent provisions contained in these Acts for individual and business taxpayers.

Note: Keep in mind that the Appendix B material only highlights the most important changes in these new laws.

Appendix A

Due Diligence Checklist

Due Diligence

For the purchase of a business to be successful, there can be no room for surprises. A review of the business being acquired needs to be done to determine if there is anything that should be known before the deal takes place. The following Checklist provides an outline of the types of documentation and information that should be reviewed. Of course, this is only a guideline; every industry and each business will have its own peculiarities and will necessitate adjustments to the list.

Sample Due Diligence Checklist

1. **Corporate documents**
   - ☐ Copies of incorporation, bylaws, and shareholder agreements.
   - ☐ Stock ledgers, including information on all outstanding stock.

2. **Contracts and agreements**
   - ☐ Recent copies of all employment, consulting, and compensation contracts, agreements, plans, and programs.
   - ☐ Details on all related party receivables or payables.
   - ☐ Recent copies of all retirement plan documents.
   - ☐ Copies of all noncompete agreements.
   - ☐ Details on all related-party receivables or payables.
   - ☐ Details on any (prior) owners who have left the firm within the last five years.

3. **Client matters**
   - ☐ List of clients lost in the last three years, client billings and reason for the loss.
   - ☐ For the last three years, a list of the top ten current clients in fee billing; percent of standard, nature of services, and how long with the firm.
   - ☐ List of the top ten new clients and their current status with the firm in terms of billing, receivables, and satisfaction.
   - ☐ List of major proposals that are outstanding, including budgeted standard and fee quoted.
   - ☐ List of aged accounts receivable.

4. **Reputation and litigation**
    - ☐ Files on any known or anticipated litigation.
    - ☐ Copies of all correspondence pertaining to litigation matters.
    - ☐ Inquiries of local sources on firm reputation.

5. **Firm stability**
    - ☐ Owners—List of all owners who have left in the last five years and the circumstances behind the departure.
    - ☐ Staff—List of managers and other key client contacts who have left in the last three years, the circumstances including how much client volume left because of the departure.

6. **Insurance coverage**
    - ☐ Copies of all current insurance policies.
    - ☐ Copies of all recent correspondence from insurance companies.

7. **Credit and related documents**
    - ☐ Copies of all agreements, bank lines of credit, and other debt obligations.
    - ☐ Copies of all material financing documents, such as capitalized leases and installment transactions.
    - ☐ Copies of all material guarantees, indemnifications, or loans.
    - ☐ Credit and reference checks on all owners.

8. **Real estate**
    - ☐ Copies of all deeds, mortgages, title policies on property owned.
    - ☐ Copies of all leases.
    - ☐ Copies of all insurance policies related to property owned.

Appendix B

Summary* of Provisions of The Working Families Tax Relief Act of 2004 and the American Jobs Creation Act of 2004

Legislative Developments

Summary of Provisions of the Working Families Tax Relief Act of 2004 and the American Jobs Creation Act of 2004

In October 2004, President Bush signed both the Working Families Tax Relief Act of 2004 (WFTRA) and the American Jobs Creation Act (AJCA) of 2004. Both Acts contain provisions that affect businesses, as well as individuals. The following is a brief explanation of the pertinent provisions contained in these Acts for individual and business taxpayers. Please keep in mind that this summary merely highlights the most important changes in these new laws.

Individual Provisions

Child Tax Credit

The child tax credit, which is $1,000 per child for 2004 but was scheduled to drop to $700 for 2005 through 2008 and to rise to $800 for 2009, will stay at $1,000 through 2010.

Marriage Penalty Relief

Two provisions that provide a measure of relief from the marriage penalty are extended. The provision setting the standard deduction for joint filers at twice that of single taxpayers, and the provision that increases the size of the 15% rate bracket for married couples filing joint returns, both of which were due to expire at the end of 2004, are extended through 2010.

Source: UHY Advisors (see www.uhy-us.com). Reprinted with permission.

Ten Percent (10%) Bracket

The scheduled reduction in the amount of income subject to the 10% tax bracket is repealed, effective through 2010.

Higher Exemption Amount Extended

In recent years, Congress has provided a measure of relief from the Alternative Minimum Tax (AMT) by raising the AMT "exemption amounts," thereby reducing the likelihood of an AMT liability. However, this partial relief was set to expire for tax years beginning after 2004, and the exemption amounts were scheduled to revert to the lower amounts allowed under prior law. The Act preserves this partial relief from the AMT by extending the higher exemption amounts to 2005.

Deduction of State and Local General Sales Taxes

In a move that will primarily benefit individuals in states with sales taxes but with no or limited individual income taxes, (i.e., AK, FL, NV, NH, SD, TN, TX, WA and WY), taxpayers, who can itemize their deductions, will be able to deduct on their federal tax returns for 2004 and 2005 either what they pay in state and local income taxes or what they pay in sales taxes (typically, the greater of the two). Previously, only state and local income tax payments were deductible. Taxpayers who itemize may deduct their actual sales taxes or use IRS published tables. Taxpayers opting to use the IRS tables will have the ability to also deduct sales taxes for certain "big ticket" items such as boats, vehicles and other items to be listed by the IRS.

Limitations on Charitable Deductions of Vehicles

Generally, no deduction will be allowed for the contribution of a vehicle, unless the contribution is substantiated by a contemporaneous written acknowledgement from the donee organization containing certain information and certification(s), and the acknowledgement is included with the tax return on which the deduction is claimed. The amount of the deduction will be limited to the gross sales proceeds, should the organization sell the vehicle without any significant intervening use or material improvement.

Non-Qualified Deferred Compensation

The AJCA makes it difficult for plan participants to defer tax on non-qualified deferred compensation for amounts deferred in tax years beginning after 2004. If at any time during the year, a plan does not meet certain operational standards, the participant must recognize all income deferred from the current and prior years.

Appendix B

Business Provisions

Repeal of Exclusion For Extraterritorial Income

At the heart of the AJCA is the repeal of the exclusion for Extraterritorial Income (ETI). Specifically, the AJCA repeals the ETI system of tax benefits for transactions after 2004, with transition relief for 2005 and 2006 and grandfather rules for contracts entered into before Sept. 18, 2003.

New Deduction For U.S. Production Activities

The AJCA replaces ETI with a new tax break for domestic production activities. The deduction is a percentage of the net income from those activities—3% in 2005-2006, 6% for 2007-2009, 9% after 2009. (The 9% deduction percentage is intended to be equivalent to a 3% rate cut).

The U.S. production activities deduction is allowed with respect to a taxpayer's qualified production activities income, which is the taxpayer's domestic production gross receipts net of expenses. "Domestic production gross receipts" are receipts derived from the following:

- Any lease, rental, license, sale, exchange, or other disposition of:
    - qualifying production property (i.e., tangible personal property, any computer software, and certain sound recordings manufactured, produced, grown, or extracted in whole or in significant part by the taxpayer within the U.S.;
    - any qualified film produced by the taxpayer; or
    - electricity, natural gas, and potable water produced by taxpayers in the U.S.
- Construction performed in the U.S.
- Engineering and architectural services performed in the U.S. for construction projects in the U.S.

The deduction is available to all taxpayers with qualified production activities income. For passthrough entities (such as S corporations and partnerships), the deduction generally is determined at the shareholder or partner level by taking into account their proportional share of the qualified production activities income of the entity.

Tax Reform and Simplification For U.S. Businesses With Foreign Earnings

The AJCA includes several provisions to reduce double taxation of U.S.-based companies, including reducing the Foreign Tax Credit (FTC) baskets from nine to two and allowing FTCs to be carried forward for 10 years instead of five.

The AJCA repeals the 90% limitation on the use of FTCs against AMT.

The AJCA encourages companies to reinvest foreign earnings in the U.S. by temporarily allowing an 85% dividends-received deduction on distributions from controlled foreign corporations.

Adviser's Guide to Tax Consequences of the Purchase and Sale of a Business

Business Tax Incentives

The Acts have a number of business related incentives including:

- an extension for two years the increased Code Section 179 expensing so qualifying businesses can immediately expense over $100,000 (with indexing) of new investments through 2007.

- 15-year write-off for qualifying leasehold improvements and restaurant property.

- 10 provisions that make it easier for businesses to qualify and operate as an S corporation, including raising the maximum number of shareholders from 75 to 100 and allowing family members to be counted as one shareholder.

- limiting the amount of the cost of an SUV that may be expensed in a single year to $25,000, effective for vehicles placed in service after October 22, 2004.

- an extension of the research credit, extended for amounts paid or incurred after June 30, 2004 and before 2006.

- an extension of the work opportunity tax credit and the welfare-to-work credit, extended for wages paid or incurred for individuals beginning work after 2003 and before 2006.

- an extension of the enhanced deduction for a corporation's qualified computer contributions, for contributions made in tax years beginning after 2003 and before 2006.

- suspending the net-income limitation on percentage depletion for marginal wells, effective for tax years beginning after 2003 and before 2006.

Glossary of Terms

The following is a glossary of tax terms discussed in the book.

401(k) plan – A qualified retirement plan to which contributions from salary are made from pre-tax dollars.

Accelerated depreciation – Computation of depreciation to provide greater deductions in earlier years of equipment and other business or investment property.

Accounting method – Rules applied in determining when and how to report income and expenses on tax returns.

Accrual method – Method of accounting that reports income when it is earned, disregarding when it may be received, and expense when incurred, disregarding when it is actually paid.

Acquisition debt – Mortgage taken to buy, hold, or substantially improve main or second home that serves as security.

Active participation – Rental real estate activity involving property management at a level that permits deduction of losses.

Adjusted basis – Basis in property increased by some expenses (e.g., by capital improvements) or decreased by some tax benefit (e.g., by depreciation).

Adjusted gross income (AGI) – Gross income minus above-the-line deductions (i.e., deductions other than itemized deductions, the standard deduction, and personal and dependency exemptions).

Alimony – Payments for the support or maintenance of one's spouse pursuant to a judicial decree or written agreement related to divorce or separation.

Alternative minimum tax (AMT) – System comparing the tax results with and without the benefit of tax preference items for the purpose of preventing tax avoidance.

Amortization – Write-off of an intangible asset's cost over a number of years.

Adviser's Guide to Tax Consequences of the Purchase and Sale of a Business

Applicable federal rate (AFR) – An interest rate determined by reference to the average market yield on U.S. government obligations. Used in §7872 to determine the treatment of loans with below-market interest rates.

At-risk rules – Limits on tax losses to business activities in which an individual taxpayer has an economic stake.

Backup withholding – Withholding at a rate of 31% on interest or dividend payments by a payor that has not received required taxpayer identification number (TIN) information.

Bad debt – Uncollectible debt deductible as an ordinary loss if associated with a business and otherwise deductible as short-term capital loss.

Basis – Amount determined by a taxpayer's investment in property for purposes of determining gain or loss on the sale of property or in computing depreciation.

Cafeteria plan – Written plan allowing employees to choose among two or more benefits (consisting of cash and qualified benefits) and to pay for the benefits with pretax dollars. Must conform to §125 requirements.

Capital asset – Investments (e.g., stocks, bonds, and mutual funds) and personal property (e.g., home).

Capital gain/loss – Profit (net of losses) on the sale or exchange of a capital asset or §1231 property, subject to favorable tax rates, and loss on such sales or exchanges (net of gains) deductible against $3,000 of ordinary income.

Capitalization – Addition of cost or expense to the basis of property.

Carryovers (carryforwards) and carrybacks – Tax deductions and credits not fully used in one year and chargeable against prior or future tax years.

Conservation Reserve Program (CRP) – A voluntary program for soil, water, and wildlife conservation, wetland establishment and restoration and reforestation, administered by the U.S. Department of Agriculture.

Credit – Amount subtracted from income tax liability.

Deduction – Expense subtracted in computing adjusted gross income.

Defined benefit plan – Qualified retirement plan basing annual contributions on targeted benefit amounts.

Defined contribution plan – Qualified retirement plan with annual contributions based on a percentage of compensation.

Glossary

Depletion – Deduction for the extent a natural resource is used.

Depreciation – Proportionate deduction based on the cost of business or investment property with a useful life (or recovery period) greater than one year.

Earned income – Wages, bonuses, vacation pay, and other remuneration, including self-employment income, for services rendered.

Earned income credit – Refundable credit available to low-income individuals.

Employee stock ownership plan (ESOP) – Defined contribution plan that is a stock bonus plan or a combined stock bonus and money purchase plan designed to invest primarily in qualifying employer securities.

Estimated tax – Quarterly payments of income tax liability by individuals, corporations, trusts and estates.

Exemption – A deduction against net income based on taxpayer status (i.e., single, head of household, married filing jointly or separately, trusts, and estates.

Fair market value – The price that would be agreed upon by a willing seller and willing buyer, established by markets for publicly-traded stocks, or determined by appraisal.

Fiscal year – A 12-month taxable period ending on any date other than December 31.

Foreign tax – Income tax paid to a foreign country and deductible or creditable, at the taxpayer's election, against U.S. income tax.

Gift – Transfer of money or property without expectation of anything in return, and excludable from income by the recipient. A gift may still be affected by the unified estate and gift transfer tax applicable to the gift's maker.

Goodwill – A business asset, intangible in nature, adding a value beyond the business's tangible assets.

Gross income – Income from any and all sources, after any exclusions and before any deductions are taken into consideration.

Half-year convention – A depreciation rule assuming property other than real estate is placed in service in the middle of the tax year.

Head-of-household – An unmarried individual who provides and maintains a household for a qualifying dependent and therefore is subject to distinct tax rates.

Health savings account (HSA) – Tax-exempt trust or custodial account established exclusively to pay qualified medical expenses of the account beneficiary who, for the months for which contributions are made to an HSA, is covered under a high-deductible health plan.

Holding period – The period of time a taxpayer holds onto property, therefore affecting tax treatment on its disposition.

Imputed interest – Income deemed attributable to deferred-payment transfers, such as below-market loans, for which no interest or unrealistically low interest is charged.

Incentive stock option (ISO) – An option to purchase stock in connection with an individual's employment, which defers tax liability until all of the stock acquired by means of the option is sold or exchanged.

Income in respect of a decedent (IRD) – Income earned by a person but not paid until after his or her death.

Independent contractor – A self-employed individual whose work method or time is not controlled by an employer.

Indexing – Adjustments in deductions, credits, exemptions and exclusions, plan contributions, AGI limits, etc., to reflect annual inflation figures.

Individual retirement account (IRA) – Tax-exempt trust created or organized in the U.S. for the exclusive benefit of an individual or the individual's beneficiaries.

Information returns – Statements of income and other items recognizable for tax purposes provided to the IRS and the taxpayer. Form W-2 and forms in the 1099 series, as well as Schedules K-1, are the prominent examples.

Installment method – Tax accounting method for reporting gain on a sale over the period of tax years during which payments are made, i.e., over the payment period specified in an installment sale agreement.

Intangible property – Items such as patents, copyrights, and goodwill.

Inventory – Goods held for sale to customers, including materials used in the production of those goods.

Involuntary conversion – A forced disposition (e.g., casualty, theft, condemnation) for which deferral of gain may be available.

Jeopardy – For tax purposes, a determination that payment of a tax deficiency may be assessed immediately as the most viable means of ensuring its payment.

Glossary

Keogh plan – A qualified retirement plan available to self-employed persons.

Key employee – Officers, employees, and officers defined by the Internal Revenue Code for purposes of determining whether a plan is "top heavy."

Kiddie tax – Application of parents' maximum tax rate to unearned income of their child under age 14.

Lien – A charge upon property after a tax assessment has been made and until tax liability is satisfied.

Like-kind exchange – Tax-free exchange of business or investment property for property that is similar or related in service or use.

Listed property – Items subject to special restrictions on depreciation (e.g., cars, computers, cell phones).

Lump-sum distribution – Distribution of an individual's entire interest in a qualified retirement plan within one tax year.

Marginal tax rate – The highest tax bracket applicable to an individual's income.

Material participation – The measurement of an individual's involvement in business operations for purposes of the passive activity loss rules.

Medical savings account (MSA) – A savings plan providing for deduction of contributions, tax-deferred earnings, and exclusion of tax on any monies withdrawn for medical purposes.

Mid-month convention – Assumption, for purposes of computing depreciation, that all real property is placed in service in the middle of the month.

Mid-quarter convention – Assumption, for purposes of computing depreciation, that all property other than real property is placed in service in the middle of the quarter, when the basis of property placed in service in the final quarter exceeds a statutory percentage of the basis of all property placed in service during the year.

Minimum distribution – A retirement plan distribution, based on life expectancies, that an individual must take after age 70½ in order to avoid tax penalties.

Minimum funding requirements – Associated with defined benefit plans and certain other plans, such as money purchase plans, assuring the plan has enough assets to satisfy its current and anticipated liabilities.

Adviser's Guide to Tax Consequences of the Purchase and Sale of a Business

Miscellaneous itemized deduction – Deductions for certain expenses (e.g., unreimbursed employee expenses) limited to only the amount by which they exceed 2% of adjusted gross income.

Money purchase plan – Defined contribution plan in which the contributions by the employer are mandatory and established other than by reference to the employer's profits.

Net operating loss (NOL) – A business or casualty loss for which amounts exceeding the allowable deduction in the current tax year may be carried back 2 years to reduce previous tax liability and forward 20 years to cover any remaining unused loss deduction.

Nonresident alien – An individual who is neither a citizen nor a resident of the United States and who is taxed on income effectively connected with a U.S. trade or business.

Original issue discount (OID) – The excess of face value over issue price set by a purchase agreement.

Passive activity loss (PAL) – Losses allowable only to the extent of income derived each year (i.e., by means of carryover) from rental property or business activities in which the taxpayer does not materially participate.

Pass-through entities – Partnerships, LLCs, LLPs, S corporations, and trusts and estates whose income or loss is reported by the partner, member, shareholder, or beneficiary.

Personal holding company (PHC) – A corporation, usually closely-held, that exists to hold investments such as stocks, bonds, or personal service contracts and to time distributions of income in a manner that limits the owner's tax liability.

Qualified subchapter S trust (QSST) – A trust that qualifies specific requirements for eligibility as an S corporation shareholder.

Real estate investment trust (REIT) – A form of investment in which a trust holds real estate or mortgages and distributes income, in whole or in part, to the beneficiaries (i.e., investors).

Real estate mortgage investment conduit (REMIC) – Treated as a partnership, investors purchase interests in this entity, which holds a fixed pool of mortgages.

Realized gain or loss – The difference between property's basis and the amount received upon its sale or exchange.

Recapture – The amount of a prior deduction or credit recognized as income or affecting its characterization (capital gain v. ordinary income) when the property giving rise to the deduction or credit is disposed of.

Glossary

Recognized gain or loss – The amount of realized gain or loss that must be included in taxable income.

Regulated investment company (RIC) – A corporation serving as a mutual fund that acts as investment agents for shareholders and customarily dealing in government and corporate securities.

Reorganization – Restructuring of corporations under specific Internal Revenue Code rules so as to result in nonrecognition of gain.

Resident alien – An individual who is a permanent resident, has substantial presence, or, under specific election rules is taxed as a U.S. citizen.

Roth IRA – Form of individual retirement account that produces, subject to holding period requirements, nontaxable earnings.

S corporation – A corporation that, upon satisfying requirements concerning its ownership, may elect to act as a pass-through entity.

Saver's credit – Term commonly used to describe §25B credit for qualified contributions to a retirement plan or via elective deferrals.

Section 1231 property – Depreciable business property eligible for capital gains treatment.

Section 1244 stock – Closely held stock whose sale may produce an ordinary, rather than capital, loss (subject to caps).

Split-dollar life insurance – Arrangement between an employer and employee under which the life insurance policy benefits are contractually split, and the costs (premiums) are also split.

Statutory employee – An insurance agent or other specified worker who is subject to Social Security taxes on wages but eligible to claim deductions available to the self-employed.

Stock bonus plan – A plan established and maintained to provide benefits similar to those of a profit-sharing plan, except the benefits must be distributable in stock of the employer company.

Tax preference items – Tax benefits deemed includable for purposes of the alternative minimum tax.

Tax shelter – A tax-favored investment, typically in the form of a partnership or joint venture, that is subject to scrutiny as tax-avoidance device.

Tentative tax – Income tax liability before taking into account certain credits, and AMT liability reduced regular tax liability.

Transportation expense – The cost of transportation from one point to another.

Travel expense – Transportation, meals, and lodging costs incurred away from home and for trade or business purposes.

Unearned income – Income from investments (i.e., interest, dividends, and capital gains).

Uniform capitalization rules (UNICAP) – Rules requiring capitalization of property used in a business or income-producing activity (e.g., items used in producing inventory) and to certain property acquired for resale.

Unrelated business income (UBIT) – Exempt organization income produced by activities beyond the organization's exempt purposes and therefore taxable.

Wash sale – Sale of securities preceded or followed within 30 days by a purchase of substantially identical securities. Recognition of any loss on the sale is disallowed.

Index

5

5% Shareholders 5-1, 5-2, 5-3, 5-5, 5-6, 5-7, 7-4, 7-5

A

About the Author... ix
Acquisition of a Business from a LLC...................... 6-15
Acquisition of a Business from an S Corporation........... 6-2
Acquisitions from a Sole Proprietorship 6-1
Allocation xi, 2-3, 2-11, 2-12, 2-13, 2-14, 2-15, 2-16, 2-17, 2-18, 3-1, 3-2, 3-9, 4-3, 4-6, 4-7, 6-1, 6-3, 6-6, 7-2, 8-4, 8-5
Allocation of Purchase Price......................... 2-11, 2-12, 3-9
American Jobs Creation Act of 2004 .... xii, 9-4, B-1, B-2, B-3, B-4
Amortization xi, 2-2, 2-11, 2-21, 3-1, 3-2, 3-3, 3-4, 3-7, 3-9, 3-10, 4-2, 4-4, 4-8, 6-4, 8-2
Asset Acquisitions 2-2, 2-12, 4-3, 4-6, 5-12, 7-1
Asset Purchases 1-2, 3-9, 4-2, 7-1
Asset Transactions – Buyer Concerns............................. 2-2
Asset Transactions – Seller Concerns............................. 2-2
Asset Versus Stock Sale 6-5
Assets Purchase 1-2, 2-14

B

Built-in Gains and Losses 5-8, 5-9

C

Compensation Issues.. 8-1, 8-5
Continuing Partners 6-11, 6-12, 6-15
Corporate Liquidations 2-2, 2-3
Customer-Based Intangible.............................. 3-4, 3-5, 3-6

D

Drawbacks 2-2, 4-3
Due Diligence .... xii, 1-2, 8-3, 8-4, A-1, A-2

E

Election 1-3, 2-2, 2-12, 4-1, 4-3, 4-4, 4-5, 4-6, 4-7, 4-8, 4-10, 4-11, 5-11, 6-2, 6-3, 6-4, 6-5, 6-6, 6-11, 6-13, 7-1, 7-2, 7-3, 8-2, 8-5
Equity Structure Shifts 5-2
Excess Depreciation on Real Property 2-9
Excluded Assets 3-7
Expenses Incurred in an Acquisition 8-1, 8-5
Expensing vs. Capitalizing... 8-2

F

Form 8023 .... 7-2, 7-3, 7-11
Form 8308 .... 6-8, 7-3, 7-4, 7-9
Form 8594 .... 2-17, 2-27, 7-1, 7-2
Form 8883 .... 7-2, 7-3, 7-13

G

Gain 1-3, 1-6, 1-7, 2-2, 2-3, 2-4, 2-5, 2-6, 2-7, 2-8, 2-9, 2-10, 2-11, 2-12, 3-2, 3-3, 3-8, 3-9, 4-1, 4-2, 4-3, 4-4, 4-5, 4-6, 4-8, 5-8, 5-9, 5-11, 5-12, 5-13, 6-1, 6-3, 6-5, 6-6, 6-7, 6-8, 6-9, 6-13, 6-14, 6-15, 8-11
Gain on Asset Sale 6-3
Greenmail .... xii, 8-1, 8-5, 8-6, 8-10, 8-11, 8-12

I

Information Base 3-4, 3-5
Installment Sales 2-9, 2-10, 2-18
Intangible Assets ... xi, 2-11, 3-1, 3-2, 3-3, 3-4, 3-7, 3-10, 3-11, 8-5

L

Liquidation Distributions 2-3, 2-8
Loss Corporation Information Disclosure 7-4
Losses Limited by §382 5-3

I-1

O

Overview xi
Owner Shifts 5-2

P

Partnership...xi, 1-1, 1-4, 2-1, 3-7, 3-9, 6-1, 6-2, 6-6, 6-7, 6-8, 6-9, 6-10, 6-11, 6-12, 6-13, 6-14, 6-15, 7-1, 7-2, 7-3, 7-4
Partnership Interests.....6-6, 6-7, 6-8, 6-9, 6-11, 6-12, 6-13, 6-15, 7-1, 7-3, 7-4
Passive Income Limitation... 6-3
Purchase of a Partnership Interest 6-7, 6-15
Purchase of Assets from a Partnership 6-6
Purchaser..1-3, 1-4, 1-5, 1-6, 2-11, 2-12, 2-14, 2-17, 2-18, 3-10, 3-11, 4-1, 4-2, 4-3, 4-4, 4-5, 4-7, 4-8, 5-13, 6-3, 6-4, 6-7, 6-10, 6-11, 6-12, 7-1, 7-2, 7-3, 8-2, 8-4

R

Recapture 1-3, 2-8, 2-9, 2-10, 2-11, 2-18, 6-9
Related Costs 2-17, 8-4
Reporting Requirements..xii, 2-17, 2-18, 4-6, 6-6, 6-8, 7-1, 7-2
Requirements for Section 338 Treatment 4-3

S

S Corporation Assets 6-3
S Election.. 6-2, 6-3, 6-4, 6-5
Sale or Exchange 2-4, 2-10, 6-10, 6-12, 7-1, 7-3
Section 1060.....2-2, 2-3, 2-11, 2-12, 2-13, 2-16, 2-17, 2-18, 3-2, 3-12, 4-3, 4-6, 4-7, 6-1, 6-3, 6-6, 6-7, 7-1
Section 197 Intangibles............. 2-14, 3-5, 3-6, 3-7, 3-8, 3-9
Section 269 .... 5-10, 5-11, 5-13
Section 382...4-4, 5-1, 5-2, 5-3, 5-4, 5-5, 5-6, 5-7, 5-8, 5-9, 5-11, 5-12, 5-13, 7-1, 7-4, 7-5

Section 383 .... 5-9, 5-13
Section 384 .... 5-11, 5-12, 5-13
Seller 1-1, 1-3, 1-4, 1-5, 1-6, 1-7, 2-1, 2-2, 2-3, 2-9, 2-10, 2-11, 2-12, 2-14, 2-17, 2-18, 3-2, 3-3, 3-9, 4-2,, 4-5, 4-6, 4-8, 6-1, 6-3, 6-6, 6-7, 6-8, 6-9, 7-1, 7-2, 7-3
Separate Return Limitation Years (SRLYs). 5-9, 5-10, 5-13
Special Rules .... xi, 1-4, 2-5, 2-8, 3-8, 3-9, 5-5, 5-8, 6-11
Stock ....xi, 1-2, 1-3, 1-4, 1-5, 1-6, 1-7, 2-2, 2-3, 2-4, 2-6, 2-7, 2-10, 2-12, 2-14, 2-18, 3-4, 4-1, 4-2, 4-3, 4-4, 4-5, 4-6, 4-7, 4-8, 5-1, 5-2, 5-5, 5-6, 5-7, 5-10, 5-11, 5-12, 5-13, 6-2, 6-3, 6-4, 6-5, 7-1, 7-2, 7-4, 7-5, 8-2, 8-4, 8-5, 8-6, 8-10, 8-11,
Stock Acquisitions 2-2, 4-2, 4-7, 4-8, 5-1, 5-12
Stock Purchases......................... 1-3, 4-2, 4-3, 5-13, 7-1, 7-2
Stock Sale..... 1-2, 1-3, 1-4, 1-6, 4-2, 4-3, 4-4, 4-6, 4-8, 6-3, 6-4, 6-5
Subsequent Adjustment 2-17
Supplier-Based Intangible 3-6

T

Takeovers 8-2, 8-4, 8-10
Tax Attributes xi, 1-3, 1-6, 2-2, 4-1, 4-2, 4-3, 4-4, 4-5, 4-6, 4-8, 5-1, 5-13
Tax Consequences...xii, 1-3, 1-4, 1-7, 2-1, 2-3, 2-7, 2-8, 2-17, 3-3, 4-1, 4-2, 4-5, 4-6, 4-7, 5-10, 6-1, 6-2, 6-3, 6-13, 6-14, 6-15, 8-6
Taxable Stock Sale vs. Taxable Asset Sale 4-2
Taxable Stock Transactions .... xi, 4-1
Taxable vs. Tax-Free 1-5 1-7
Termination 6-4, 6-6, 6-13
Testing Periods 5-1, 5-2
Treating Stock Purchases as Asset Purchases 4-2

W

When to Use Section 338 Election 4-6
Workforce 3-4, 3-5
Working Families Tax Relief Act of 2004...xii, 9-4, B-1, B-2, B-3, B-4
Written Agreement, Effect of 2-17